HOW TO LAUNCH AND MARKET A BOOK

The Sixth Month Countdown

Dr. Melissa Caudle

Absolute Author
Publishing House

New Orleans, Louisiana

Absolute Author
Publishing House

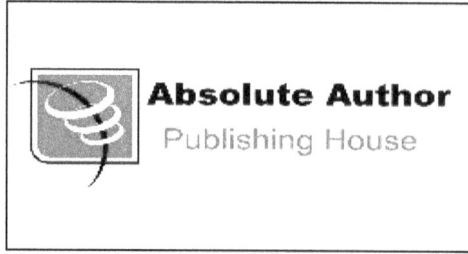

www.absoluteauthor.com

How to Launch and Market Your Book
Copyright 2019
Dr. Melissa Caudle

This book nor the author can guarantee that your book will sell or launch as the #1 New Release. It is based from the experience of the author, but you will get a return based on your individual efforts. Also, Dr. Melissa Caudle is not an attorney nor a certified public accountant and cannot give financial or legal advice. Comments in those areas are for educational purposes only.

Publisher: Absolute Author Publishing House
Editor Supervisor: Dr. Carol Michaels
Proof Editor: Kathy Kittok
Line Editor: Erin Wright
Copy Editor and Audiobook Editor: Timothy Burke
Focus Group: Rory White, Thomas Higgins, Dr. L. A. Davis, Alicia Manafort, Sophie Wright, Connie Radcliff, and Tymothy Burke
Author Photographer: Robby Cook Stroud
All Graphics: On the Lot Productions
Front and Back Cover Design: Rebecca at Rebeccacovers

Printed in the United States of America. All rights reserved, including the right to reproduce this book or portions thereof in any form whatsoever. Contact author at drmelcaudle@gmail.com *or* www.drmelcaudle.com.

Library of Congress Cataloging-in-Publication Data
Caudle, Melissa.
    How to Launch and Market Your Book / Dr. Melissa Caudle
        p. cm.
ISBN: 978-1-7337182-2-6

1.   Reference   2. Writing and Research

DEDICATION

To all the authors in the world because of their love of writing. May you reach your goal and continue to author novels for the rest of your life.

SPECIAL THANKS

To author a book inspiration must come from somewhere. Ideas don't come freely, and my dreams usually inspire my novels. For this book, I had a dream too, not when I slept, but my desire to launch my book Never Stop Running as the #1 New Release on Amazon to honor my mother. For that to happen, I had to apply marketing strategies. I want to thank several people who inspired me to write this book for other authors. Without them requesting how I consistently launch my books as the #1 New Release, this book would not have been written, so I want to say thank you to them.

I also want to thank my focus group members Rory White, Thomas Higgins, Dr. L. A. Davis, Alicia Manafort, Sophie Wright, Connie Radcliff, and Timothy Burke who not only tested the strategies I presented in this book but also for their feedback.

To my talented group of editors Dr. Carol Michaels, Kathy Rabb Kittok and Timothy Burke thank you for your eagle eyes. I especially want to point out that Timothy Burke not only helped to edit this book but also edited the audiobook version and will be narrating the audiobook. Thank you, Timothy.

TABLE OF CONTENTS

INTRODUCTION

PREPARE TO LAUNCH AS THE #1 NEW RELEASE

As an author you dream of writing a best-selling novel. I know because I did too, but for this to happen it takes months of preparation before launching your book. There is no need to worry because I'm going to guide you through the process of how I pre-launched my books and marketed them. I cannot guarantee this process will work for you, but I can say it worked for me.

When I launched my novel *Never Stop Running* (NSR), it released as the #1 New Release on Amazon. Releasing at the top doesn't happen by happenstance; it happened because of the months of preparation and marketing I did in advance. To make things more complicated for me, three months earlier I launched *The Keystroke Killer: Transcendence* (KSK). I learned a thing or two during that process. I will admit that KSK did not open as the #1 New Release, but it finally made it to the Top 100 list coming in at #45 after I researched how to market a book. In my case, hindsight outweighed foresight. Had I known what I know

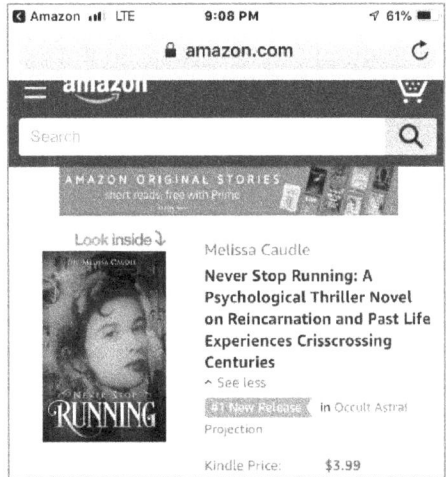

now, KSK would have launched as the #1 New Release. Now I apply the lessons I learned as I prepare to launch A.D.A.M. See, I am already pre-launching and pre-marketing my next novel, and I haven't finished the rough draft.

The Keystroke Killer: Transcendence - A Serial Killer Action Packed Psychological Thriller Kindle Edition

by Dr. Melissa Caudle ~ (Author)

★ ★ ★ ★ ★ ~ 7 customer reviews

› See all 2 formats and editions

Kindle	Paperback
$0.00 kindleunlimited	$14.99
Read with Kindle Unlimited to also enjoy access to over 1 million more titles	2 Used from $14.46
$0.00 to buy	4 New from $14.53

New Orleans · 2058 · MATTHEW RAYMOND, a private detective, locked into a maze of deceit and deception uncovers the truth of Project Transcendence. A gripping page-turning thriller serial killer novel in the tradition of "The Silence of the Lambs," "Darkly Dreaming Dexter," and "Misery" that demands to be read. One part suspenseful thriller of 'who done it,' one part science fiction and one part sizzling erotica that makes "Fifty Shades of Grey" look PG. "The Keystroke

I will admit that I wasted too much money, probably a couple of grand, on marketing KSK. Frankly, I didn't know what I was doing. I learned and adapted quickly, and I don't make the same mistakes twice. Although I have published numerous non-fiction books, the marketing strategies I used for them were different and ineffective for fiction. My editor, Dr. Carol Michaels, informed me of that. One would think there would be tons of information available on the internet on how to launch a fiction book.

Wow! Watch out! There are a ton of scams that will zap your money all in the name of book launching and book promotion. I learned the hard way. I came across several websites that I thought I would find the information on how to launch a book. You know the ones, sign up to the blog and receive a free eBook; the result, a twelve-page PDF file to encourage me to register for a seminar. I registered for the workshop, but the only thing I learned about launching a book was that the creator would coach me for a price and schedule an appointment for a one on one free consultation. I did, he called. Our conversation left me with no more information on launching and marketing a book that I didn't already know other than if I wanted specifics I would have to enroll in his webinar – cost $299. Here is how our conversation went.

Mel: I don't want to enroll in a webinar. I want to read it and put the book in my reference library. Do you have a book I could buy?

Him: I have a book, but it just skims the surface. What you're looking for I tell you in my webinar. Would you like to go ahead and register for it?

Mel: I don't want to participate in a webinar. I want something to read. I'm old-fashioned that way.

Him: Well, you're a writer, then write one yourself.

Mel: Great idea, thank you. When you see it, you'll know the moment I received my inspiration to write it.

That conversation sent me on my journey to learn how to launch and market a book. It was too late for *The Keystroke Killer*, but I had *Never Stop Running's* first draft complete. So, I kept researching, researching, and I took an online course in marketing strategies from a local university. Senior citizenship in Louisiana has its advantages. The moment you turn sixty you can enroll in any Louisiana Public University and take courses or get a degree for free. Although I have a Ph.D., I will always continue to learn. That one course changed my entire direction on launching and marketing a book. I am currently on my fourth course in marketing. In this book, you will learn about my book launch and marketing strategy.

I also learned that if I spent between thirty minutes to an hour each day on my marketing strategy, I could boost my books to the top and so can you.

One of the cool aspects of this book is that I have also included checklists at the end of every chapter to get you organized and keep you on task to launch and market your book. I strongly advise that you use them.

Myths About Book Launches

Authors seem to be under the impression that if you write a book and publish it on Amazon or Kobo, readers will purchase it and read it. I'm sorry to say it doesn't work that way. If readers don't hear of it or know of it, they pass over it. The moral of this story is that you must get the word out about your book long before the launch.

Another myth is that if you traditionally publish, it is the publisher's job to promote and prepare your book for the launch. Are you kidding? Some publisher's do market your book, but not to the extent that you as an author will. The quicker you believe this, the better prepared you will be to launch and market your book. It is my opinion that if you don't plan on your book to sell, then don't plan to market it – at all. To do so is ludicrous. As an author you spend months on end developing your novel, why not put the same amount of time into marketing it so that it can bring you potential income. You must spend money to make money on your book.

Remember You are a Business

The moment you decided to author a book, you became an entrepreneur. That means you must treat your writing as a business. Any expenses you incur from launching your book to marketing your book are tax deductible, so remember to keep all receipts. As I am not a tax advisor, I cannot offer you tax advice as what you can or cannot deduct on your income tax return. Please consult with a lawyer or CPA as to the best way to handle your taxes because you will also have to pay taxes on your royalties.

Are you ready to jump right in and prepare to launch and market your book? I hope so because the information in this book could change your writing career.

1. SIX MONTHS BEFORE LAUNCH

One of the most challenging things for an author once he or she finishes the first draft of their book is to know when and how to market it. We were born to be writers, not marketers. However, writers must become marketers if they stand a chance of competing with the millions of other books published. I am here not only to guide in launching your novel but also to identify how to market it to become the #1 New Release. This book contains step-by-step actions which spread across six months. As an author would you author your novel without the appropriate tools? I think not. Then why market your book without them? You shouldn't as your launch and marketing strategy will not be effective without the correct tools, and you will waste valuable money and your time.

What I have learned to recognize is that there are three types of authors:

1. **"I'll write it, and they'll read it" author** – this is the mindset of an author who doesn't recognize that they are a brand that they must market. Chances are they never break below the top one hundred sellers on Amazon.

2. **"I don't know how so I'll pay out the nose blindly" author** – this is the mindset of an author lost in the marketing arena. They know they are going to have to market their book, so

they pay publicists, social influencers and buy expensive advertisements not knowing if they will ever achieve the outcome of a best-selling author. They have no idea about branding themselves as an author.

3. **"I've got a plan" author** – this is the mindset of an author who plans their book launch and strategically markets their book. I believe those who fail to plan, plan to fail. This author understands that not only they must brand themselves as an author, but they also must prepare to launch and market their books.

If you purchased this book, chances are you have been in the mindset of author one or two, and you're sick of spending your money as if it grew on the tree in your front yard. Hence, you're ready to make your plan not only to brand yourself as an author but also to market your books. Let's jump right into it.

SIX MONTHS BEFORE BOOK LAUNCH

Launching and marketing your book should start at least six months in advance by branding yourself as an author. You read this correctly, just like automobile companies, shoe polishes, soda companies, and coffee brands who have a recognizable brand. Whether you want to accept this or not, you as an author are a brand. The main reason for branding yourself as an author is to increase awareness. Once you are known as an author, the more you write, the more books you will sell.

First Step to Branding

The first step to branding yourself as an author is to start building your author platform from the moment you decide to publish a book. Yes, this takes time, but it's worth it. For you to develop your branding platform, it is necessary to have an author website. Your website will be your all in one go-to for your fans, and your future sells. It is best to have it completed at least six months before launching your book.

Your website should include:

- **A Landing Page** – identifies you as an author.

- **About the Author Page** – a bio that you should always have ready.

- **Contact Form or Contact Information** – so people can ask you questions.

- **A Page Dedicated to Each Book** – provides an effortless way to purchase your book.

- **Upcoming Releases** – I hope you're not going to be a one and done author because the more books you publish, the more money you will make. Duh! On a serious note, you establish a fan base the more books you publish and the stronger your fan base, the easier your next book is to sell.

- **Opt-in Mailing List** – Keep in contact with your readers and start an email list. As you write and publish more books, you will have an automatic email list to use to promote it. The easiest way I have found is to use MailChimp. It is free for the first 2,000 subscribers. Then, once a week, send an email. Please don't push your book, let it sell itself. However, share other things like book reviews, your book tour or author a short story. They also like to get to know you so share milestones in your writing. I write reviews on restaurants I've eaten in and movies I've seen. I also post on my attendance to the New Orleans Saints games.

Look at my landing page for my website: www.drmelcaudle.com. Notice that I brand myself as an author and I have dedicated pages. When anyone goes to my site, there is no doubt that I am an author. I have also made it easy for them to purchase my books.

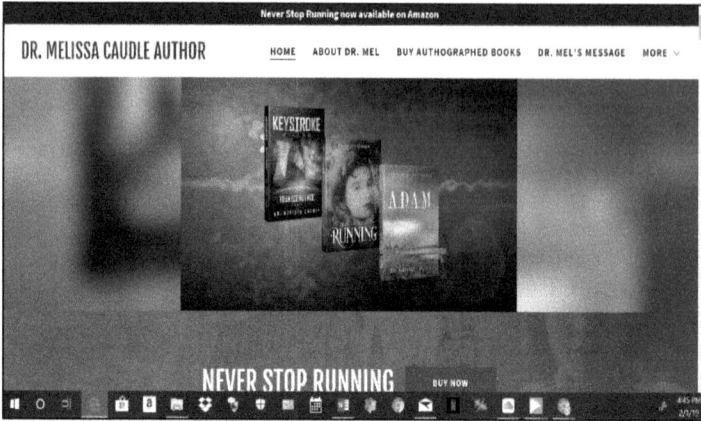

What you don't see are the tabs beneath the "More" tab. When you scroll over it, you can go to individual pages for each of my books, my upcoming releases, contact me page, Dr. Mel's Book Club, and more. I also took the advantage to begin advertising my new novel *Never Stop Running* on the top mini black banner. At the time of this writing, I promoted *Never Stop Running* on the top banner, but within weeks, it'll change to read – *"A.D.A.M.* Launch Date Coming Summer of 2019*,"* and as I write more novels, I will modify the banner to announce my new upcoming books. Also notice that at the time of this writing, A.D.A.M. was in the editing stage, but I already had the cover for it and included it on my landing page to brand myself.

There are a variety of ways for you to obtain a website. I know money is always tight, but there are free options and well as inexpensive options. I use Godaddy.com for my author website. I find that the platform is inexpensive and easy to manipulate. I also purchased my domain name from them and bought the hosting package.

Another free alternative is Blogger. I know what you're thinking; it's for a blog. Well, kinda sorta. Yes, you can blog on it, but if you're not a blogger or have no intentions of ever becoming one, you can design your BlogSpot like a website, and it's free. Look at the next picture below. Notice that it looks like a website with a navigation menu. It's not my website; it's my blog. The best news is that it is free.

WordPress is also a fantastic site to start an author website, and it is free too. I find it to be more cumbersome to use. You can sign up to use their hosting and purchase a domain if you want to go that route. Later, when you need to sell your books, you can upgrade to the business plan.

Now if you want to have immediate recognition as an author, my publisher, Absolute Author Publishing House at www.absoluteauthor.com offers free interviews to authors as a way to advertise your book. If you don't have a webpage, you can still have your information available and use that link. The beauty of this for a minimal fee, you can have your interview on a dedicated sub-page with a link. During your early branding process, I advise for you to complete this author interview.

Second Step to Branding

I have already touched on this subject, but an excellent way to start branding yourself as an author is to write a blog. If you don't want to maintain a blog the second-best alternative is to become a guest blogger.

The key is to start establishing your fan base which becomes essential in the marketing phase. You can guest blog on mine at:

www.drmelcaudle.blogspot.com

Third Step to Branding

Social media plays a huge role today. Everything is at our fingertips, and you can become known because of it. As an author, it is essential for you to hone your social media skills, but the first step is to have a social media presence.

To brand yourself as an author on social media, I recommend that you establish an account on:

- Facebook
- Instagram
- Twitter
- Pinterest
- LinkedIn
- Goodreads
- BookBub

Even before you publish, have your accounts ready for action. The goal is to build connections by joining writing groups, attend conferences, and to join professional organizations.

Your Cover

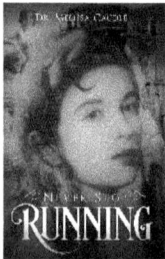

Six months out from your book's launch, it is necessary for you to have your book's cover design. Without it, you can't get it embedded into the mind of potential buyers. Readers are visual people. It's one thing for me to say that my next book *Never Stop Running* will launch in six months, but what if I gave a visual? Your future readers will retain that visual of your cover.

For each of my books, I have the covers completed long before I've finished writing them. Additionally, I have logos for each title which is another way of branding yourself. Here is the logo for *Never Stop Running*.

I want you to notice that the logo matches the book's title. I did this on purpose to brand that novel. Six months before I released this book, I blasted this logo as an upcoming novel. One week later I did a cover reveal and exploded the book's cover on all my social media sites, in my blog, and to my email subscribers. To continue this brand, I created a *Never Stop Running Regression Journal* and a *Never Stop Running Dream Journal*. The logo for these journals did not change, and I continued with the montage theme to brand each as a part of this series. These journals add to my potential buyer and fan base. They also provide opportunities for fans of the book to have something else from me. You got it, all in the name of branding and marketing.

The coolest part about the journal is that I use the back matter to provide a free excerpt from the novel. That way if someone buys one of the journals, I introduce them to the novel. After I authored those two books, I put the ads in the back matter in the novel and started cross-promoting the books.

Here is the ad for the regression journal so that you can examine the branding and cross promotion.

Next is my cover reveal graphic for my book *The Keystroke Killer: Transcendence*. Notice several things about this graphic: you clearly can see the title, you get a glimpse of what a reader thinks about the book, you know where you can purchase it, and I have a call to action that identifies my website and a giveaway for my upcoming novel.

To top it off, because *The Keystroke Killer* is a series of novels, I've already branded those novels and have the covers which I display on my website.

If you aren't a graphic designer, there are many avenues for you to have your cover designed. Research your alternatives on freelance sites such as Fiverr and Zeerk. Both are incredibly reasonable and provide an excellent quality of work. Once on Fiverr, search for Rebecacovers. She is the best and designs all of mine.

Draft Your Book's Synopsis

Six months out, your book's synopsis should be polished. I strongly advise you not to wait until the last minute to write it.

Once written, use it to market and launch your book in the following ways.

- Include on the back jacket
- Include it in press releases
- Include it on your book's sub-page on your website
- Post it to your social media sites
- Use it on sell sheets
- Use on ads

The next photograph is of a synopsis style ad for my novel A.D.A.M.

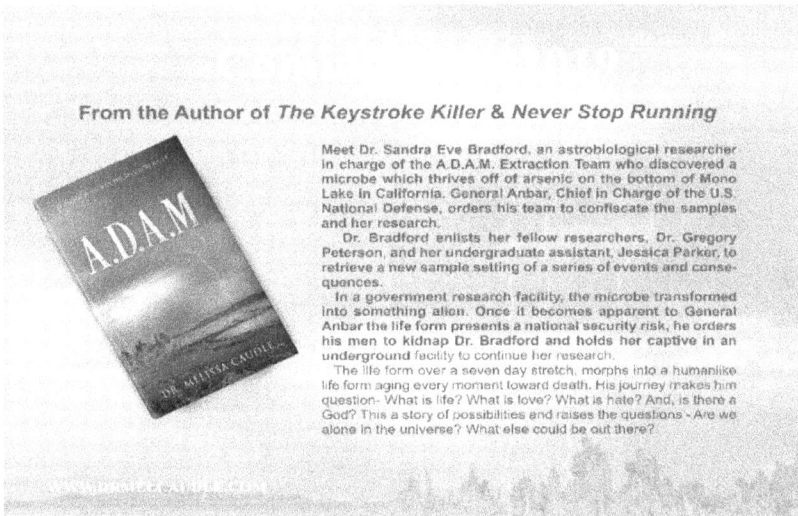

From the Author of *The Keystroke Killer* & *Never Stop Running*

Meet Dr. Sandra Eve Bradford, an astrobiological researcher in charge of the A.D.A.M. Extraction Team who discovered a microbe which thrives off of arsenic on the bottom of Mono Lake in California. General Anbar, Chief in Charge of the U.S. National Defense, orders his team to confiscate the samples and her research.

Dr. Bradford enlists her fellow researchers, Dr. Gregory Peterson, and her undergraduate assistant, Jessica Parker, to retrieve a new sample setting of a series of events and consequences.

In a government research facility, the microbe transformed into something alien. Once it becomes apparent to General Anbar the life form presents a national security risk, he orders his men to kidnap Dr. Bradford and holds her captive in an underground facility to continue her research.

The life form over a seven day stretch, morphs into a humanlike life form aging every moment toward death. His journey makes him question- What is life? What is love? What is hate? And, is there a God? This a story of possibilities and raises the questions - Are we alone in the universe? What else could be out there?

Edit Your Manuscript Six Months Out

Please do not make a mistake and edit your book on your own. Although I have a Ph.D., I'm a professional editor, and I'm an author, I still don't edit my manuscripts. I hire it out. Please do not wait until the last minute because you are going to need a clean version to send to your beta readers and the last thing you want to do is to give them a poorly edited version. Additionally, once your manuscript is polished six months in advance, it allows you to rest your mind from the writing aspect and plan your pre-sale marketing campaign ads. That's right, pre-sales. I provide more information on this in another section.

Don't rely on your friends or family to serve as your editor. Why? Simply stated, although they have your best interest in mind, they are neither trained nor experienced in editing. A bad editing job may as well be a no editing job. When you make mistakes in the editing process, your book will not sell.

I discovered as a professional editor with Absolute Author Publishing House many authors do not understand the distinct types of editors; so, I'm going to explain the difference so you can decide on the best editing service you need.

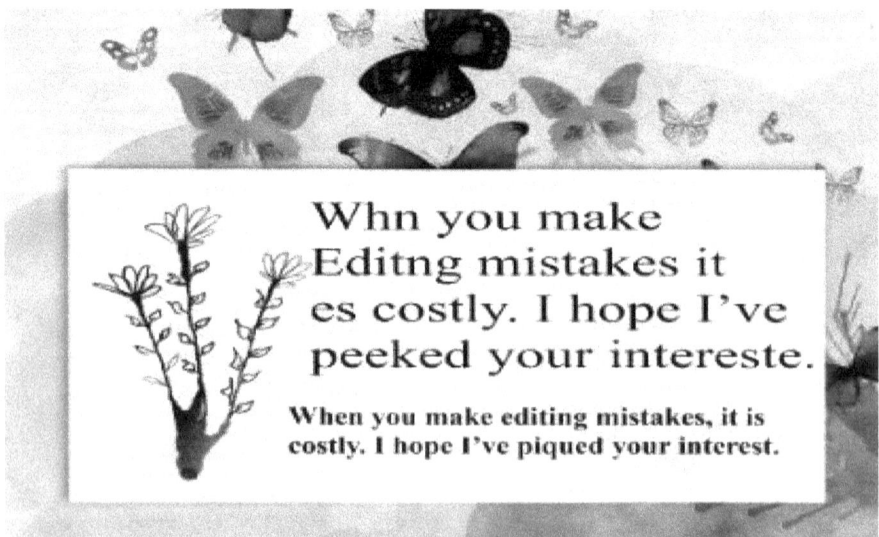

Whn you make Editng mistakes it es costly. I hope I've peeked your intereste.

When you make editing mistakes, it is costly. I hope I've piqued your interest.

HOW TO LAUNCH AND MARKET A BOOK

1. **Copy Line Editor** – Copy editors or proof editors review and edits your manuscript to correct grammar and sentence structure. They have a keen eye for errors. They do not rewrite your manuscript, but rather correct your mistakes in punctuation, spelling, and grammar.

2. **Line Editor** – A line editor will do the job of a copy editor but will also make recommendations to improve the flow of ideas and to resolve inconsistencies. They see the big picture in a manuscript and determine whether the manuscript fits together logically and will highlight and in some cases rewrite sentences or paragraphs.

3. **Development Editor** – Developmental editors work closely with the author to hash out characters, plots, and subplots so the book flows. They will often help the author to develop the arcs in the novel. Once you work with a development editor, you will still need a line or copy editor before publication.

4. **Project Editor** – A project editor works with an author from the beginning to the end to keep them on track. They often serve as both a developmental and proof editor as well as help make decisions on book covers, trailers, and marketing tools through publication in paperback and eBook. Project editors are by far the most expensive.

5. **eBook Editor** – An eBook editor converts your manuscript into an eBook format. To compete in today's market, you will need your book to be in both paperback and eBook. We have several experienced editors who can convert your manuscript into an eBook. Book our services below.

6. **Audible Editor/Producer** – An Audible Editor produces your book into an audible book. This type of editor handles everything from finding the perfect voice to produce your audible book to get it market ready.

Any editor you hire, make sure they offer their service in Microsoft Word and provide tracked changes and comments. I always ask for a sample edit first by sending the first couple of pages before I hire them because I want to see if they are any good at what they edit. Below is a sample tracked copy of what I did for my novel A.D.A.M. to show those of you who may night be aware of what to look for from an editor.

The two agents escorted Dr. Bradford from the lab as Rebecca, George and Jessica chased after them. The door shut behind them.

In a few seconds, Jessica re-entered the lab, turned off the lights and quickly closed the door behind her.

The murky water in one of the five tubes glowed neon yellow as the water vibrated.

Rebecca stood in front of the building ready to transmit a live broadcast to KWNC as both Agents and Dr. Bradford entered the black government sedan.

"Good morning. I'm Rebecca Newcombe and this is the KWNC Morning News. The top story of the day comes to us from the N.A.E.T. Research Facility in New Orleans, Louisiana. Just a few minutes ago, Dr. Sandra Bradford was taken into custody by the FBI. At the time, I was in the process of interviewing Dr. Bradford in her lab when the two arresting agents entered and demanded her presence at FBI headquarters. It is not clear if Dr. Bradford is being charged with any criminal activity or if she is a suspect in the death of Dr. Gregory Peterson. It has only been three weeks since the scientific team, led by Dr. Bradford discovered the new life form that thrives off of arsenic known as A.D.A.M. The acronym means Arsenic Driven Astrobiological Microbe. This historic discovery changes the way the scientific community identifies life as we now know it."

As the black sedan pulled away, Jessica gazed out the lab's window and observed. She huffed as a scowl developed deeply across her brow. "They can't do this to her."

Melissa Caudle	You needed to show and not
Melissa Caudle	Deleted: back …
Melissa Caudle	Deleted: the station…
Melissa Caudle	Deleted: the…
Melissa Caudle	Deleted: get into a…
Melissa Caudle	Deleted: B…
Melissa Caudle	Deleted: SUV…
Melissa Caudle	Deleted: as…
Melissa Caudle	Deleted: is…
Melissa Caudle	Deleted: ing…that
Melissa Caudle	Deleted: that …
Melissa Caudle	Deleted: she…goes with them
Melissa Caudle	Deleted: goes with them to …

Melissa Caudle A few seconds ago
This area was boring and needed more than the black SUV left. Notice how I added action and dialogue to enhance. It is now "show" and not a telling sentence.

SIX MONTHS BEFORE LAUNCH CHECKLIST

Branding Yourself as an Author

Create a Website
Be sure it includes the following elements.

- Landing Page
- Author Page
- Contact Form
- Contact Info
- Dedicated Book Page
- Upcoming Releases
- Opt-In Mailing List
- Blog
- Press & Media Page

NOTES

Create a Blog Website

- Completed
- Draft First Blog

Create Accounts on Social Media

- Facebook
- Instagram
- Twitter
- Pinterest
- LinkedIn
- Goodreads
- BookBub

NOTES

Cover Design

○ Completed
○ Cover Design Reveal onto Social Media

Synopsis Written and Polished

○ Post on Website
○ Create a Synopsis Ad
○ Post on Social Media Sites

Hire an Editor

○ Vet the Editors
○ Tracked Changes Received
○ First Draft Edited

NOTES

2. FIVE MONTHS BEFORE LAUNCH

Now that you have your first draft in decent shape and your synopsis developed, five months from launch date it's time to create your marketing plan. As dull as it sounds, you need an action plan on who and where to market your book. It is your road map. How are you going to know when you've arrived if you don't know where you're going? Your marketing plan will guide you every step of the way. Now here is the best part, once you create one marketing plan, the next one is easier because you will have an outline or template to follow. Listed below are thirteen steps to develop your marketing plan.

Step 1 - Define Your Audience

Whom you think your audience is and who they are, do not go hand-in-hand. You must be target specific and know your audience. Consider two of my books, *The Keystroke Killer* and *Never Stop Running*. Those books are as opposite as night and day; therefore, two different audiences. I know this. A reader who purchases *The Keystroke Killer* expecting *Never Stop Running* to be like it, has a shock coming. I'm very honest with my readers about this. Before I recommend them to a potential buyer, I let them know what they will find.

Please do not tempt yourself to skip this step as your target audience guides everything else in your marketing plan. I wouldn't target readers of romance novels with an ad for *The Keystroke Killer*. I'd waste my

19

money. Why would I target science fiction lovers with my next book *Secret Romances: A Forbidden Thirst for Love?* The way to find your target audience is to do a little investigating on your own. Visit Facebook, Goodreads, Amazon, and Pinterest and make a note of the audience who reads your book's genre. You might find that women between the ages of thirty-five and fifty read romance novels. What about serial killer books? Find out the age group and plan to target them with your ads. The key to discovering your target group is to ask, "Who will purchase my book?"

Step 2 - Identify Your Retail Price of Your Book and How You Will Fulfill Orders

If you price your book correctly, it will sell. The price you set is a touchy subject for most authors because they always feel their book is worth a lot more than the average selling price of a book in their genre. I felt that way because I spent a year developing a book, and now I can only charge $12.99 for the paperback and $3.99 for my eBook. That's not a big payoff.

To identify your retail price, go to Amazon or Barnes & Noble websites and identify twenty books on your subject matter and in your genre. Do some old-fashioned math and average the prices. That is your starting point for your novel. I always choose an amount just under the average position to give myself more room to attract buyers.

Now that you know how much to set your retail price, now decide how to fulfill your orders. Are you going to publish on Kindle or Kobo? Will you go the traditional route of publishing? It would behoove you to determine this factor because it will also direct your marketing campaign.

Step 3 - Identify Your Audience's Hang Outs

The places where your audience hangs out are the places where you should target your ads and where social media is a key contributor. Join Facebook groups and interact with others. I don't mean start pitching your book but contribute to it. Get your name out there. Brand yourself as an author.

Now if your audience isn't on Facebook, as some aren't, find out where they hang out on the internet. I discovered various chat rooms on the topics of my books and developed relationships. I didn't have to market my book because people looked up my website and or went to my blog. They appreciated the fact that I didn't push my books and I interacted as a peer.

Once you identify these hangouts, they become the places you will want to run ads.

Step 4 - Decide on Your Marketing Budget

Face the fact you are going to spend money to launch and market your book. You can't avoid it. The two things you have control of are how much you spend and where you spend it. When I began writing, I set aside twenty dollars a week into my marketing savings account. It added up quickly, but I spent it just as fast. It would be best if you made this a priority. Choose your amount and start saving toward your goal even if it means giving up a store-bought coffee or taking your lunch to work instead of spending money. In other words, learn to budget your marketing expenses.

Step 5 - Identify Blogs to Be a Guest Blogger

I can honestly say I follow several dozen bloggers because it keeps me involved and for the most part, I obtain some useful information and tidbits. Identify as many blogs as possible that your target audience is interested in or follow, reach out, and ask if you can guest blog on their site. I guest blog all the time, and I invite any reader of this book to reach out to me if you are interested in guest blogging. My blog is:

www.drmelcaudle.blogspot.com

Blog by Dr. Mel Caudle
Dr. Mel's Message
Subscribe to Dr. Mel's Blog!

Step 6 - List Five Topics You Could Blog

Now that you identified blogs identify five topics and write your posts. It is essential to have them ready, so when you contact bloggers, you can share what you want to share and offer to email your post for pre-approval. If you don't have them pre-written, you might find yourself in a jam. Spend this month and prepare as many blog posts as possible. Who knows, you might decide to start a blog of your own which I do recommend as an action step during your pre-launch. Blog post ideas:

- How to Overcome Writer's Block
- Writing Prompts to Get Your Daily Writing Habit Started
- Why I Became a Writer
- Authors Who Influenced You
- How to Handle Rejection Letters
- Why I Chose to Self-Publish
- Influencing a Character's Dialogue with Action
- Use of Strong Action Verbs
- Authoring Thoughts for Your Characters

Step 7 - Identify Your Launch Team Members

When you launch a book, you need all the help you can get. Spend time to develop a list of people you know who will be willing to share your announcements on their social media sites. The more people on the list, the better. My launch team included my editors, beta readers, daughters, sisters, and about ten of my friends. To effectively use launch team members, create a private group on Facebook or a private email group to keep in contact and to keep them updated.

Step 8 - Identify Ten People to Write a Review

Reviews! They are hard to come by but attainable. Write a list of people who will write you a review on Amazon or Goodreads. My first choice is my launch team members and beta readers.

Step 9 - List Your Marketing Tools You Want to Use

Marketing your book without marketing tools is hard. Identify the ones you want.

Step 10 – Identify Ways to Grow Your Email List and Subscribers

One of the most prominent marketing strategies that is free is developing an email list. Identify how you are going to grow yours and make it a point to communicate often to keep their interest. Examples include:

- Give an excerpt if they subscribe
- Give them a list of ten sites to publish press releases
- Give them a short story
- Give them a free bookmark

Step 11 – Identify Endorsers for Your Book

As a first-time author it isn't going to be easy to find someone to endorse your book, but don't let that stop you from trying. During this month, draft a letter of introduction and write to those whom you think would be an excellent endorser. For my book *Never Stop Running* I reached out to famous regression hypnotherapists. I wouldn't dare ask them to endorse *The Keystroke Killer*. I went to other crime novelists. Again, this all turns back to your target audience.

Step 12 - Identify Journalists to Interview You

In this step, you are going to identify local journalists from your hometown newspaper and television stations. You need to gather their email address and telephone numbers which takes time, and you want the list ready at any stage when you have a press release.

If you make contact early, they'll remember your name when you launch your book.

Step 13 - Commit to Perseverance

It takes a long time to write, launch and market a book. Be prepared to persevere. In your marketing plan add actions steps to help you.

Here is my Marketing Action Plan for *Never Stop Running*.

NEVER STOP
RUNNING

MARKETING ACTION PLAN

Target Audience

Men and Women – 30-63 with an interest in reincarnation
Men and Women – 30-63 with an interest in memoirs
Regression subjects of any age
Hypnotherapists

Retail Price: Paperback: $12.99 eBook $3.99

Fulfillment of Orders

- Amazon
- Kindle
- Autographed Copies

Audience's Hang Outs

- Facebook
- Goodreads
- BookBub
- Chat Rooms
- Instagram

Marketing Budget

- Facebook Ads - $200
- Goodreads Ads - $200
- Amazon Ads - $400
- Press Releases - $10
- Marketing Tools - $30

Blogs to Be a Guest Blogger

www.drmelcaudle.blogspot.com
www.absoluteauthor.com
www.pastlivestoday.com
www.mindfulnesscreation.com

www.awakentoday.com
www.herewego.com
www.Shortstories.com

Topics to Blog

1. Using Your Past Life Regression to Overcome a Phobia
2. Dealing with a Soulmate
3. Dealing with Conflictions in Your Religion
4. Working Through the Fear of Dying
5. My Past Life Regression Session
6. Why Keeping a Journal Helps

Launch Team Members

1. Erin
2. Mike
3. Jay
4. Kelly
5. Michelle
6. Robby
7. Caylen
8. Tina
9. Carol
10. Alfred
11. James K.
12. James C.
13. Roger
14. Helen R.

Potential Professional Reviewers

- Dr. Carol Michaels
- Susan L.
- Dr. Charles Ellis
- Regina Whitmore
- Candance Baylor
- Kirkus

Marketing Tools

- Flipbook Trailer
- Cinematic Trailer
- Teaser Trailer
- Bookmarks & Cards
- Sell Sheet
- Graphic Designed Ads

Grow Your Email List and Subscribers

- Weekly Blog
- Guest Blog

- Giveaways
- Public Speaking at Rotary Clubs etc.
- Author Career Days at Schools

Possible Endorsers

- Dr. Brian Weiss
- Dr. Charles Ellis

Journalists for Interview

- News with a Twist
- Carol Livingston
- Hoda Kobe

Note: Your action plan does not have to be long or detailed. The goal is to get you organized and focused on the task to launch and market your book.

FIVE MONTHS BEFORE LAUNCH CHECKLIST

Create Your Action Plan

Step 1 - Define Your Audience

- Age
- Demographics
- Male
- Female
- What are their interests?

Describe your Target Audience:

_____

_____

Step 2 - Retail Price

- Search Amazon

Identify five books like yours and record the price.

1. _____

2. _____

3. _____

4. _____

5. _____

What is the average price for the above books? _____

Identify your projected retail price for your book. _____

Step 3 – Audience Hangouts

o Facebook
o Instagram
o Twitter
o Pinterest
o LinkedIn
o Goodreads
o BookBub
o Other

NOTES

Step 4 – Budget

o Editing
o Cover Design
o Pre-Launch Graphics
o Launch Graphics
o Ads
o Launch Party
o Book Tours

Step 5 – Blogs to Guest Post

o www.drmelcaudle.blogspot.com/
o www.absoluteauthor.com

Step 6 – Topics to Blog About

o Identify five topics you can blog.

    1. _____

    2. _____

    3. _____

    4. _____

5. _____

Step 7 – Identify Launch Team Members

1. _____
2. _____
3. _____
4. _____
5. _____
6. _____
7. _____
8. _____
9. _____
10. _____

Step 8 – List of Potential Book Reviewers

1. _____
2. _____
3. _____
4. _____
5. _____
6. _____
7. _____
8. _____
9. _____

10. _____

☐ Step 9 – Market Tools Needed

○ Flipbook Trailer
○ Bold Trailer
○ Teaser Trailer
○ Bookmarks
○ Business Cards
○ Sell Sheet
○ Graphic Design Ads

☐ Step 10 – Describe Methods to Grow Your Subscriber's List

1. _____
2. _____
3. _____
4. _____
5. _____
6. _____
7. _____
8. _____
9. _____

☐ Step 11 – Identify Possible Endorsers

○ Completed
1. _____
2. _____
3. _____

4. _____

Step 12 – Identify Journalists to Interview You

Collect Names and Contact Information.

1. _____
2. _____
3. _____
4. _____
5. _____
6. _____
7. _____
8. _____
9. _____
10. _____

Step 13 – Commit to Perseverance

○ Completed

3. FOUR MONTHS BEFORE LAUNCH

F our months might sound like it is a lot of time to get ready for your launch, but it isn't. The time will fly by because you are going to be extremely busy making sure your manuscript is ready for publication, setting a date for the launch and obtaining your marketing tools.

Set Your Launch Date

You are four months out, and it is time to decide on your launch date. Here is some advice on choosing the date. Don't select one that conflicts with a best-selling author's new novel launch date. Do choose a date your audience will probably remember.

There are three hundred and sixty-five days in a year. You only must choose one. I select my publishing dates around holidays because those dates are easy for readers to remember. I launched *The Keystroke Killer* on October 31, 2018, which was Halloween. My audience could remember that. I chose January 19, 2019, to publish *Never Stop Running* to honor my mother who graced the cover because it was her eighty-fifth birthday. To create a buzz around this date, I used social media to let everyone know my mother was on the cover and why it was important to me. She dreamed of being a cover model her entire life; then she was diagnosed with stage four lung cancer. I made her dream come true. What I didn't know was how my audience was going to react. When the book came out, I received hundreds of requests for not only for my autograph but also for my mother's.

Design Marketing Materials

Now that you have your launch date you must design and create your marketing tools. I use Art Publishing Pro to design my ads after I purchase a gig on Fiverr that provides me mock-up cover ads. I buy one hundred different ones because from the moment I receive them I post one a day to my social media accounts announcing the launch of my new book.

What you have done is announced the pre-launch date but be advised that Amazon doesn't allow you to start the actual pre-orders until three months before publication. I pre-launch my book on Amazon for pre-sales. I modify the ads by placing my targeting wording on them to announce the launch, the pre-sale, exclusive contests, or giveaways, and more. I do this because I have three months of sales before the book goes live. The day it goes live, all pre-sales count as sales on launch day, and this boosts my book to the top. That is why it is important not to wait too long before offering your book for pre-sale.

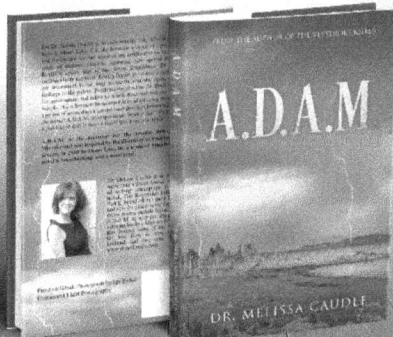

PRE-ORDER NOW ON AMAZON.COM

One Scientist. One Alien Lifeform. Consequences for Mankind.

When a scientist discovers a microbe in Mono Lake California, the scientific community must rethink the definition of life as the microbe morphs into something unimaginable setting of one of the largest government conspiracy.

A.D.A.M

DR. MELISSA CAUDLE

"One of the most thrilling novels to date from Dr. Melissa Caudle." Erin W.

"This could really happen. What else could be out there?" Monica F.

"To think the science behind this is real gave me chills." George H.

Available June 2019

When you have finished that, it is time to either create or update your author profiles and biographies on your social media accounts.

Masterfully write your bio as exciting as you can. Use this bio to brand yourself. It goes on your website, in your book, and on your author social media websites.

Here is a list of author pages you should create and maintain for the rest of your author days.

- Facebook Business Page for Book
- Author Facebook Page
- Goodreads Author Profile
- Amazon Author Profile
- Website Author Page
- BookBub Author Page
- Netgalley
- Pinterest
- Linkedin
- Instagram
- YouTube

Must-Have Marketing Tools

Trust me when I say I feel your pain; marketing is a necessary evil in the life of a book author. Are you kidding me; we were born to write and not born to market? Your daily chore to launch your book is marketing. Essentially, that means you must have the marketing tools to do it. Listed below is what I consider the must-have tools to launch and market your book

- A Flipbook Trailer
- Teaser Trailer(s)
- Bookmarks
- Business Cards
- Graphic
- Sell Sheets
- Mock Cover Ads
- Arsenal of Images
- Press Releases

The Bookmark for *The Keystroke Killer*

A Sell Sheet – A sell sheet is a single document which highlights your book to give to book reviewers, newspapers, magazines, bookstores, etc. Your business card isn't effective as it does not provide the information needed. The essential items to include in your one sheet are:

- Your Name
- The Book's Name and the Book's Cover
- The Book's Genre
- Catchy Headline
- Three paragraphs

    1. Introduce yourself

    2. Introduce the Book

    3. Call to Action

- Unique Quotes from Beta Readers and Endorsers
- Contact Information
- Email address, phone number, and author website

I think it is clear as to what the sections mean that needs to be included on a sell sheet. However, the goal for you is to learn to write precise information. That means your biography and synopsis must be crisp and precise. Additionally, when you write your headline make it catchy.

The call to action area needs to be short which directs the person to do something, ideally purchase your book and join your blog as a subscriber.

On the following page, I have included a template for you to design your sell sheet. My life is made easier by using this template because I am not recreating the wheel.

After the template, I have included my sell sheets for three of my novels. Scrutinize them and notice how I followed the template and how I adjusted it to accommodate the information I desired.

NAME OF YOUR BOOK OR LOGO

Place your book's Synopsis her.

Cover

Reviews.

Book Details here

Publisher:
Date Published:
Language:
Number of Pages:
ISBN:
Size:
Paperback: $
Ebook: $
Available on Amazon Kindle

Author Photograph

Author Bio Here

WEBSITE ADDRESS HERE

To contact author for more information or for an interview call (telephone number here) or email him or her at (phone number here). To keep update on author's new releases subscribe to their blog at: www.blogsite.

A.D.A.M

Meet Dr. Sandra Eve Bradford, an astrobiological researcher in charge of the A.D.A.M. Extraction Team discovered a microbe which thrives off of arsenic on the bottom of Mono Lake in California. General Anbar, Chief in Charge of the U.S. National Defense, orders his team to confiscate the samples and her research.

Dr. Bradford enlists her fellow researchers, Dr. Greg Peterson, and her undergraduate assistant, Jessica Parker, to retrieve a new sample setting of a series of events and consequences.

In a government research facility, the microbe transformed into something alien. Once it becomes apparent to General Anbar, the life form presents a national security risk, her orders his to kidnap Dr. Bradford and holds her captive in an underground facility to continue her research.

The life form over a seven day stretch, morphs into a humanlike life form aging every moment toward death. His journey makes him question- What is life? What is love? What is hate? And, is there a God? This a story of possibilities and raises the questions - Are we alone in the universe? What else could be out there?

Dr. Melissa Caudle debuted her novel "Never Stop Running: A Novel on Reincarnation" as the #1 New Release on Amazon. She is best known for her book "The Keystroke Killer Transcendence," a psychological thriller which took her to death row to interview serial killers. Her books have received five-starred reviews in Publishers Weekly, Booklist, Goodreads and on Amazon. She also writes non-fiction guidebooks for screenwriters on how to create one pagers, write a logline, write a synopsis and more. She also has a series of adult coloring books called "Abstract Faces." Her blog, "Dr. Mel's Message," has more than 121,000 followers where she writes about myriad interests. She enjoys the city life of New Orleans along with her husband Mike and their two sidekicks, a Tuxedo cat named Meow Mix and an American Gray Shorthair named Simone. She retired from a twenty-year career in education after writing a number one best-seller on crisis management which took her worldwide as a keynote speaker to educational conferences and pursued her lifelong passion for writing. She does her best writing at her beach condo, on cruise ships, or in her sunny-patio-home office overlooking the

Paperback: 291 pages

Publisher: Absolute Author Publishing House (June 11, 2019)

Language: English

ISBN-13: 978-

Product Dimensions: 5.2 x 0.7 x 8 inches

DR. MELISSA CAUDLE
www.DrMelCaudle.com

THE KEYSTROKE KILLER

Dr. Melissa Caudle

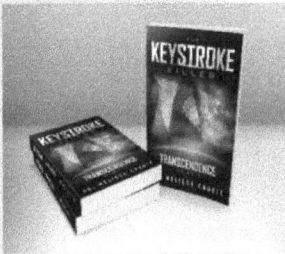

Amazon's Best Sellers Rank

Amazon Best Sellers Rank: #942 l
#41 in Kindle Store > Kindle
#69 in Kindle Store > Kindle
#125 in Kindle Store > Kindle

A modern visionary and one of the newest authors to come from America, Dr. Melissa Caudle combines a suspenseful thriller best known for her psychological thriller series "The Keystroke Killer." Other novels include "Never Stop Running" and "A.D.A.M." "Abstract Faces" Volumes 1-6 is a collection of her drawings for the adult colorist. You can follow her on her blog at www.drmelcaudle.blogspot.com.

New Orleans - 2058 - MATTHEW RAYMOND, a private detective, locked into a maze of deceit and deception uncovers the truth of Project Transcendence. A gripping page-turning thriller serial killer novel in the tradition of "The Silence of the Lambs," "Darkly Dreaming Dexter," and "Misery" that demands to be read. One part suspenseful thriller of 'who done it,' one part science fiction and one part sizzling erotica that makes "Fifty Shades of Grey" look PG, this book is an impressive debut for Caudle as she weaves her characters into a dark and twisted journey to uncover a deranged and utterly immoral serial killer who controls a weapon of mass destruction. Set in the backdrops of political corruption and scandal in 2053 New Orleans, the novel follows Matthew a tortured private investigator as he tracks down a violent and dangerous serial killer who is destined to become one of the most genuinely chilling serial killers in fiction. "The Keystroke Killer" is unforgettable and grisly disturbing you will not likely forget. This novel is not for the feint of heart, but is a must read that will keep you turning the pages as you hold your breath.

Paperback: 427 pages
Publisher: Absolute Author Publishing House (October 31, 2018)
Language: English
ISBN-13: 978-1718872561
Product Dimensions: 6.7 x 1 x 9.6 inches
Paperback: $14.99
Ebook: 6.99

www.drmelcaudle.com
Email: DrMelCaudle@gmail.com

A Flip Book Trailer

A flip book trailer is a twenty to thirty-second video that highlights the key elements in your book. These trailers are vital because they give readers a chance to look inside your book at the format and style and it's the perfect opportunity to showcase what other readers think about your book. The crucial elements of the flipbook are the title, reviewers' quotes, a peek at the pages, and when and where to purchase the book. Here are a couple of still shots from my flipbook for *The Keystroke Killer*.

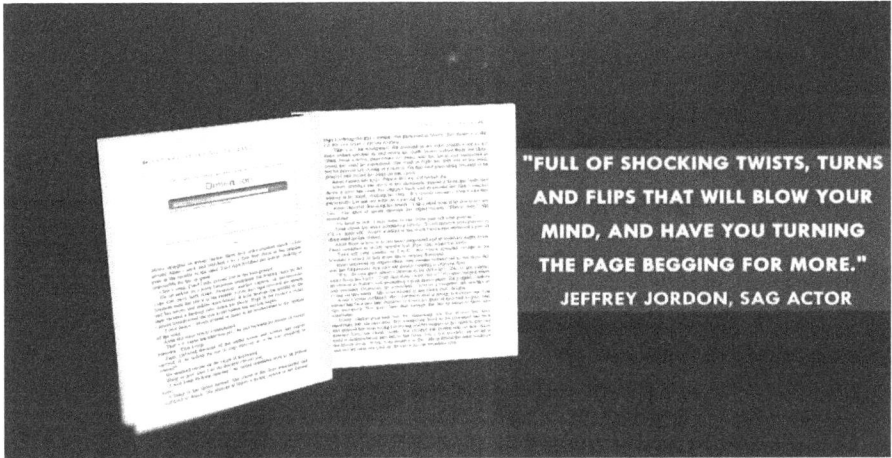

"FULL OF SHOCKING TWISTS, TURNS AND FLIPS THAT WILL BLOW YOUR MIND, AND HAVE YOU TURNING THE PAGE BEGGING FOR MORE."
JEFFREY JORDON, SAG ACTOR

A Book Trailer

Long gone are the days when someone would pick up your book based on the front cover. Yes, that is important. However, readers want to be drawn into your book visually, and a book trailer is the perfect means to accomplish this. Think of your book trailer as if it were a film. When creating a book trailer, make sure it is catchy and suits the tone and genre of your book. If you want to view my book trailers, visit my YouTube channel.

https://www.youtube.com/user/lotproducer

One thing you will find is that I have a variety of book trailers for each book. The styles target the specific audience I wanted to reach. I have cinematic, comic, trailers with dogs and cats, and more.

PRESS RELEASE TEMPLATE

Don't under-estimate the power of a press release. Not only will a press release give your book coverage while you are in pre-launch, but after it as well. During this month issue your first press release to announce the upcoming release of the book. The week after, follow that up with a press release announcing the pre-sale. Keep issuing a press release weekly until launch day. It will also get your name and your book into web search listings.

I have more than eighteen years of experience in writing and publishing press releases. What I have found is that authors have difficulty constructing two things: their synopsis for their book and their press release because they are short. So, what is the key to writing a compelling press release? Make sure to include all the elements listed below:

- The Heading & The Subtitle
- Introductory Paragraph
- The Main Body – the Who, What, When, Where, Why, etc.
- About the Author or About Us if You Have Co-authored a Book
- Contact Information

The Heading

The key to writing a compelling press release is to target your readers with a headline that is specific to your book. It must grab the attention of your reader or a journalist because that is the first thing they see. Your heading must be straight to the point and short. Writing the title is not the time to compose wordy sentences. Also, consider using a headline that is catchy to grab the reader's attention.

After that, you need a subtitle that is maybe a complete sentence that summarizes your press release.

The Introductory Paragraph

Bloggers, media influencers and journalists are remarkably busy and don't have time to read a massive amount of information. In a powerful press release, less is more. Get to the point right away and provide something interesting to keep them reading. In other words, don't include rift-raft or waffle-on with long details in your opening paragraph.

The Main Body

Now it is time to tell them about your novel. Your synopsis is excellent for this as it explains what your book's contents are. Remember to use the old-fashioned writing technique and include the who, what, where, when, and why? You could also begin or end your main body with your logline. Lastly, add the reviewer's comments and quotes.

About the Author

When you write this section, it should be boilerplate. One of the mainstays for an author is to have a compelling biography.

Contact Information

When you use a press release service, by law, you must include your contact information. For some authors, this gets a little scary because it means that they must provide their home address and phone number. Don't let that scare you as Absolute Author has a press release service that is reasonable and cost-effective. They can issue your press release under their name which will give you credibility as an author.

A Little Extra Ump!

Many press release sites don't allow the use of images; however, when you send it to journalists and bloggers, be sure to include them. I suggest you add the cover of your book and your sell sheet.

The Breakdown

I have included a press release template for you to follow. Immediately following it, I have added a press release that my publisher issued after *Never Stop Running* launched as the #1 New Release on Amazon. If all else fails, feel free to contact me, and for a small service fee, I can write one for you.

PRESS RELEASE TEMPLATE

Put an ad here

PRESS RELEASE
DATE

PUT GRABBING HEADLINE HERE

PUT SUBHEADING HERE

INTRODUCTORY PARAGRAPH

BODY

Who, What, Where, When, & Why

WHAT OTHERS ARE SAYING

ABOUT THE AUTHOR

CONTENT INFORMATION

PRESS RELEASE
January 24, 2019

NEVER STOP RUNNING DEBUTS AS #1 NEW RELEASE

Never Stop Running the novel by Dr. Melissa Caudle is her second novel and launched as the #1 New Release on Amazon.

New Orleans, LA – Absolute Author Publishing House is proud to debut a new novel, "Never Stop Running," from Dr. Melissa Caudle which launched as the #1 New Release on Amazon.

A modern visionary and one of the newest authors to come from America, Dr. Melissa Caudle combines a suspenseful thriller and the search for truth in regard to past lives and reincarnation in this mind-bending novel in the tradition of *"This Body: A Novel of Reincarnation"* by Laurel Doud, *"Journey of Souls,"* by Michael Newton, and Past Lives, *"Many Masters"* by Brian L. Weiss. The result is a masterful original fiction novel as profound as it is awe inspiring. *"Never Stop Running"* is a page-turning thriller that begs to be read in a single sitting as this mental time travel spanning centuries and numerous past lives through regression hypnotherapy unfolds. Based on a true story of one woman's struggle to recover her memories after a devastating accident left her with retrograde amnesia. This is an astonishing novel from an unforgettable author and is a must read.

What Others Are Saying

"Based on real events of regression hypnotic sessions of one brave woman, this is a tale of destiny and soul mates not to be missed. The most intriguing book you'll read all year." Dr. Carol Michaels

"You don't have to believe in reincarnation to enjoy this tale, but it will get you to thinking about the possibility." Erin Wright

"A masterful novel that keeps you engaged. A must read." Tina Rubin

ABOUT THE AUTHOR

Dr. Melissa Caudle debuted her novel Never Stop Running: A Novel on Reincarnation as the #1 New Release on Amazon. She is best known for her book The Keystroke Killer Transcendence, a psychological thriller which took her to death row to interview serial killers. Her books have received starred reviews in Publishers Weekly, Booklist, Goodreads and on Amazon. She also writes non-fiction for screenwriters, novelists or film producers and has a series of adult coloring books called Abstract Faces. She enjoys the city life of New Orleans along with her husband Mike and their two sidekicks, a Tuxedo cat named Meow Mix and an American Gray Shorthair named Simone. When she is not writing, she composes music, draws, paints, reads or edits other author's books. Her goal is to continue to live a full and rich life and write every day.

If you want to know when her next book will come out, please visit her website at http://www.drmelcaudle.com or https://www.drmelcaudle.blogspot.com where you can sign up to receive an email when she has her next release.

Distribute Your Press Release

Here's the kicker. It can get costly to issue a press release. That is where your marketing action plan comes in handy.

If you did your homework, you would already have the names and email addresses of journalists and bloggers. It's time to put it into action. As a bonus, I've included the sites that I issue my press releases through which are either free or very inexpensive. I will apologize in advance if these links are no longer available as I have no control over that.

1. https://www.prfree.org

2. http://prsync.com

3. https://hype.news/

4. http://www.postyournews.co.uk

5. https://telegra.ph

6. https://www.issuewire.com

7. https://www.newswiretoday.com/

8. https://www.media.onlineprnews.com/

9. https://www.worldnewsquest.com/submit-your-free-post

10. https://rentry.co

11. http://www.imfaceplate.com

12. https://gethermit.com/books/651415/read

13. https://justpaste.it

Create an Email Signature

A free and straightforward method to advertise your book is to create a specialized email signature which also includes your author website, a small ad about your book and a link to purchase your book or multiple books.

THIS IS A SAMPLE OF MY EMAIL SIGNATURE

Respectfully submitted,

Dr. Melissa Caudle
Author

SUBSCRIBE TO MY BLOG – Dr. Mel's Message
BUY YOUR COPY OF THE KEYSTROKE KILLER: TRANSCENDENCE

DR. MELISSA CAUDLE
AUTHOR

"If I am not writing, I'm reading. I have to say it is more than a hobby, it's my passion."

www.drmelcaudle.com

Please take note that my signature for all my emails identifies my blog, so I can obtain subscribers and links to purchase my books along with my website. My signature is free advertising for my books. Now here is another tip. I always have my vacation status on my Gmail account on which gives anyone who sends me an email an automated response telling them I will get back to them as soon as possible. Guess what? That automated response also includes my email signature. I have received sales from this technique.

BETA READERS

I cannot begin to explain how vital my beta readers are to my process. Besides your editor, your beta readers are some of the most critical people to have on your team in developing your book. They hold the key in recognizing many components that as authors we often overlook. Why? Authors are incredibly close to their manuscripts and often think they have covered something only to find out nobody understood what they meant.

I discovered many things that needed clarification. For example, I referenced something local to New Orleans. Several of my beta readers were clueless about what a Swamp Festival entailed and had no idea what Zydeco meant. I found myself adding dialogue to SHOW and not just TELL to describe these two events. I took it for granted that everyone knew that Zydeco was a form of music. I was wrong. I was quick to correct and even added my favorite Zydeco musician's new album as an ad in the back of my book.

Who Are Beta Readers?

Beta readers come from all walks of life and backgrounds. More importantly, they are individuals who love to read and are avid readers with strong opinions.

They are not editors, and they are not there to correct your spelling or catch your grammatical errors. They are readers! Therefore, to benefit from using them and their feedback be prepared to have them give you their honest opinions and feedback as if they don't, they not only have wasted your time, they have also spent theirs.

Always treat your beta readers as professionals.

Who to Enlist as Your Beta Reader?

- Bloggers with a specific interest in your genre
- Other authors with experience
- The targeted audience of readers who like your genre
- Someone who is reliable and will give honest feedback

You do not want to enlist family or friends unless they are professional beta readers. Often these two core groups won't give you the honest feedback you need.

Non-Disclosure Agreement

After I choose my beta readers, I have them sign a non-disclosure agreement to protect my unpublished material. Please know as a disclaimer I am not an attorney, and I cannot give you legal advice. Therefore, contact your attorney for your official Non-Disclosure Agreement. I am providing this sample of my non-disclosure agreement for *The Keystroke Killer Transcendence* for educational purposes only.

KSK Focus Group Non-Disclosure Agreement

Thank you for agreeing to participate in a focus group to discuss the novel THE KEYSTROKE KILLER: TRANSCENDENCE PART I in the final stages of development. The novel has ideas and concepts regarding its characters and plots and is copyright protected. The discussions here represent Confidential Information of DR. MELISSA CAUDLE / discussion ("Focus Group").

I, _____ hereby agree to maintain the confidentiality of information disclosed during focus group, the reading of the draft novel as follows:

a) To hold in confidence any and all technical or business information about THE KEYSTROKE which is disclosed, or made available to you directly or indirectly, or is information you otherwise receive incident to your participation in this discussion;

b) That any ideas, patentable or not patentable, or suggestions contributed by you during the discussion, as well as any ideas, developments, or plots conceived by you or others participating in the Focus Group, shall be the property Dr. Melissa Caudle in any manner she sees fit. Please be advised, that Dr. Caudle does not have to accept your recommendations; but, will take them under serious advisement

c) The novel, THE KEYSTROKE KILLER shown to you, described to you, and/or used by you is not available for sale at this time and no offer for sale is being made to you. You will receive your copy free for your review. Feel free to mark in it with pencil, ink, or highlighter so that you may easily identify the pages or passages you which to discuss with the author.

d) That you, shall at all times hold in trust, keep confidential and not disclose to any third party or make any use of the Confidential Information beyond those activities that are part of the Focus Group.

e) All notes, reference materials, memoranda, documentation, and records in any way incorporating or reflecting any of the Confidential Information shall belong exclusively to Dr. Melissa Caudle, and the undersigned agrees to turn over all copies of such materials in the undersigned's possession to Author upon request.

f) Also included as confidential is any participants Personally Identifiable Information ("PII"). PII shall mean a person's identity or information that might reasonably allow identification of the person. I shall at all times hold in trust, keep confidential and not disclose to any third party or make any use of the identity or PII of any Respondent involved in the Focus Group.

g) That you acknowledge you have volunteered to be a member of the KSK Focus and **will not** financially be compensated now or in the future for your participation in this Focus Group and that all information and opinions you provide are solely your own and are in no way reflective of your employer(s).

In exchange, for your participation in the KSK Focus Group, your name will be included on a Special Thanks page, along with the other focus group members, in the front of the novel recognizing you as a focus group member along with the others. The order in which your name appears will be listed in the order in which you were selected. Additionally, besides your name will be a number which represents which round of the Focus Group you participated. Lastly, you will receive an autographed copy of THE KEYSTROKE KILLER: TRANSCENDENCE PART I, from the first print.

By submitting this form, you will be entering a Non-Disclosure agreement with: DR. MELISSA CAUDLE, author, and creator of THE KEYSTROKE KILLER: TRANSCENDENCE PART I

Signature: _____

Date: _____

SEND COMPLETED FORM TO DRMELCAUDLE@GMAIL.COM
ELECTRONIC SIGNATURES ACCEPTED

■■

Please provide your current phone number, email, and address you would like for THE KEYSTROKE KILLER: TRANSCENDENCE to be sent to you.

Name: _____
Address: _____

_____
City: _____ State: _____ Zip Code: _____
Phone: _____

Email: _____

How would you like for your name to be listed on the Special Thanks Focus Group Page?

_____

Now That You Have a Beta Reader, Now What?

Round 1 – Send your manuscript to four beta readers and have them read your book. Provide the Absolute Author Beta Reader Questionnaire that I've included on the next two pages for them to take notes and make comments. Be sure to give them a deadline to complete the form and to read the book. After you receive their comments, please call them, and discuss your book. Often you will obtain valuable insight into an area that wasn't covered by the questionnaire. Take notes during your conversation so you can review them later when you make changes to your manuscript. Once that is complete, modify your manuscript.

Round 2 – Before you send your round two beta readers your new manuscript, send it to an editor again. This time a different editor. They catch things that the first editors don't. Trust me, in the end; you will get better feedback from your beta readers if they don't have to wade through typos or grammatical errors. Once edited, forward the book to your beta readers with the questionnaire and provide a deadline. Obtain their feedback, make corrections and modifications, and get ready for Round 3.

Round 3- Is a rinse and repeat of Round 2.

Round 4 – Send back your novel to the same Round 1 readers and the new Round 4 members because your Round 1 readers will be the only group to ascertain the differences and modifications you've made fully. Round 4 members will have a fresh perspective.

After you receive the feedback, modify your manuscript, and send to a professional editor or two. Again, you don't want mistakes. On the following pages is my publisher's Beta Reader Questionnaire used with permission from Absolute Author Publishing House.

TIP: Once my novel is in the hands of any beta or focus group I do not write on the contents. I put it away and draft another book or edit another author's manuscript. That's how I can publish books within months of each other. The focus groups for The *Keystroke Killer* took six weeks for each, which gave me six months to write *Never Stop Running*. So, while that book was in the beta stages, I wrote A.D.A.M. which is now in the beta stages. While I wait on that, I'm drafting Secret *Romances: A Forbidden Thirst for Love*.

BETA READER QUESTIONNAIRE

DEVELOPED BY ABSOLUTE AUTHOR

Absolute Author
Publishing House

COPYRIGHT PROTECTED 2019

Dear Beta Reader:

Thank you in advance for agreeing to beta read my latest novel. I value your input and feedback. I am supplying you with a Word Document file of the copyright document so that you can make your comments directly into the book. To accomplish this task, open Word, upload the document and click on the review section. Locate the area to track changes.

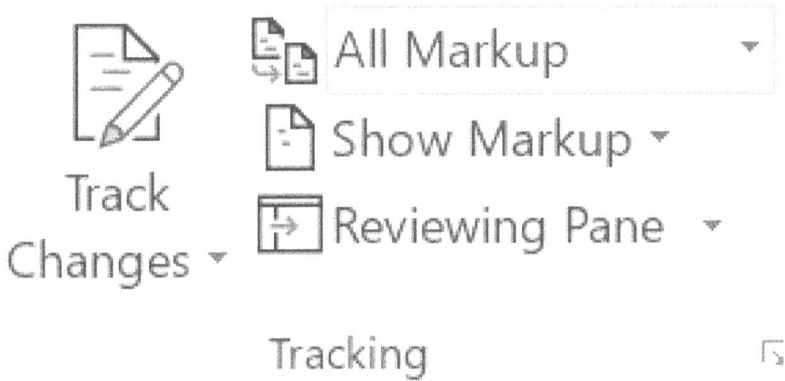

Highlight the field and click on Track Changes. After that, you will be able to use the comment section. To reach that, click on the words or sentence in the document and a menu will pop up. At the bottom, there will be the word "New Comment."

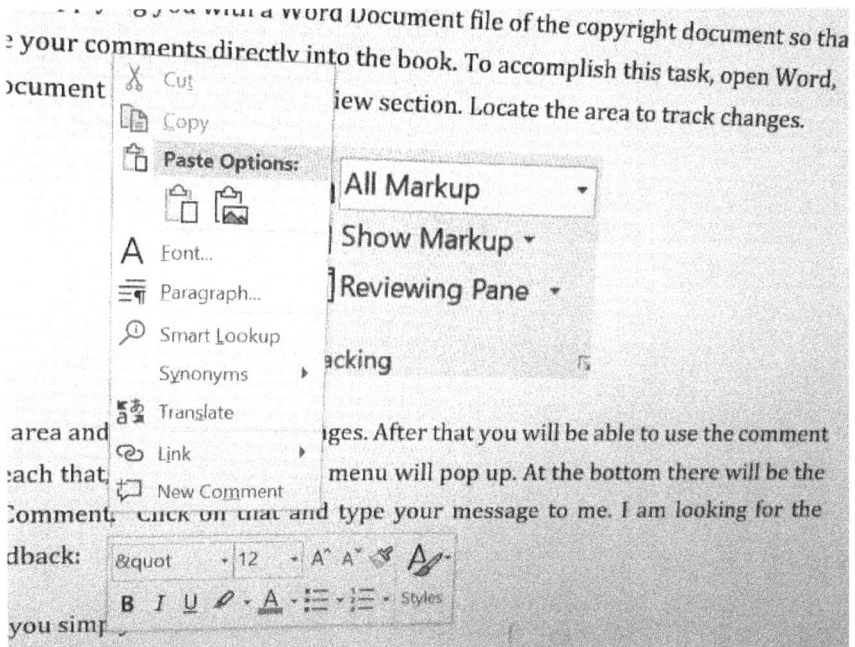

Click on New Comment and type your message to me. I am looking for the following feedback:

- Areas you simply do not understand
- Areas you like or dislike
- Areas that you feel need further development
- Redundant areas that could be omitted
- Areas that do not move the story forward
- Messy dialogue or suggested change
- Pacing

I have found this method useful for both of us. Once you have finished reading my novel, please answer these following questions and return the form to me by _____.

Once you have completed reading and making your comments, please use this form and answer the questions directly on this Word Document and return it to me. Again, I value your input and feedback.

1. Did the opening chapter catch your attention?

2. Did the opening chapter move too quickly or too slow for you?
3. What would you change about the opening chapter?

4. When it came to the setting of the book, did you get a good feel for it?

5. Was the setting consistent throughout the book?

6. What would you have liked to have been added to the setting?

7. Was the motivation of each character clear to you? If no, which character or characters need further development?

8. Were the characters believable?

9. Could you relate to the protagonist of the story?

10. Was the antagonist a formidable force?

11. Who is your favorite character and why?

12. Who is your least favorite character and why?

13. Is the plot clear?

14. Is there a part of the book that bored you and that I should remove?

15. Is there a place or concept in the book that needs more clarification?

16. Did you notice any discrepancies in the story?

17. Did you like the ending, or does it need to be changed? If it needs to change, how do you vision it ending?

18. Did you predict the ending or was it a total surprise? If yes, when what gave it away?

19. What emotions did you feel during the story? Did any make you cry, become angry, scared, etc.?

20. How would you rate this book on a scale of 1 to 10?

If you would like a PDF copy of this form, subscribe to the Absolute Author Blog and, then email carol.absoluteauthor@gmail.com and request it.

https://mailchi.mp/752e94da6e99/absoluteauthor

FAMILIARIZE YOURSELF WITH AUTHOR RESOURCES

Plenty of websites will prove beneficial for you from honing the craft of writing to marketing tools. It is imperative for you to do your research to find the ones that meet your needs. Here is a couple of my favorite.

1. **Absolute Author Publishing House** – www.absoluteauthor.com – They offer a blog with helpful tips to hone your craft and can guide you in the publication process. They have everything for you in one spot.

2. **Author's Edge** – www.adazing.com – This is a fantastic site where you can download for free a PowerPoint presentation that you can adapt for a book trailer. The templates are easy to manipulate. They also offer other services that you pay for, but I joined because they have templates for book covers, templates for book mock-ups, templates for novels, and training. I use them for my book mock-up ads which save me money in the long run.

3. **Biteable** – www.biteable.com – This website offers you the creative ability to use templates for book trailers and book ads. You can create five videos for free using thousands of high-end quality video footages. The program is easy to use, basically swap out images and titling. The catch though is that if you use the free program, it will be watermarked with their company's name. To remove the watermarks, you must subscribe which costs around $300.00. It would be best if you weighed the cost of producing a book trailer yourself or paying for one.

4. **Fiverr** – www.fiverr.com – An excellent resource to purchase freelancers to develop book trailers, mock-up ads, banners, advertisements, editors, and marketers. Just about anything that has to do with publishing a book can be found there. In fact, I offer my freelance services on this site as an editor, and I sell spots on the sidebar of my website to allow others to advertise on my site. That means I monetize my blog. Book my services through my Fiverr account below.

Here is my link on Fiverr: https://www.fiverr.com/melissacaudle

5. **Grammarly** – www.grammarly.com – Although you will still need to hire an editor, do yourself a favor and purchase Grammarly. It will keep you on track while you write.

6. **Prowritingaid** – www.prowritingaid.com – In addition to using Grammarly, I use Prowritingaid. The reason is that the two programs catch different things in writing style. To me, if they joined their programs together, it would be the perfect solution for me as an author.

FOUR MONTHS BEFORE LAUNCH CHECKLIST

Planning for the Launch

Set Launch Date

○ Completed

My launch date is: _____

Hire or Create Marketing Materials

○ Flipbook Trailer
○ Cinematic Trailer
○ Teaser Trailer
○ Bookmarks
○ Business Cards
○ Mock Cover Ads
○ Sell Sheet
○ First Press Release

Step 2. – Distribute Press Release

1. _____ https://www.prfree.org

2. _____ http://prsync.com

3. _____ https://hype.news/

4. _____ http://www.postyournews.co.uk

5. _____ https://telegra.ph

6. _____ https://www.issuewire.com

7. _____ https://www.newswiretoday.com/

8. _____ https://www.media.onlineprnews.com/

9. _____ https://www.worldnewsquest.com/submit-your-free-post

10. _____ https://rentry.co

11. _____ http://www.imfaceplate.com

12. _____ https://gethermit.com/books/651415/read

13. _____ https://justpaste.it

Email Signature

○ Email Signature Completed

Beta Reading

Identify your Beta Readers.

Collect Names and Contact Information.

1. _____
2. _____
3. _____

4. _____

5. _____

6. _____

7. _____

8. _____

9. _____

10. _____

Send Round 1 Beta Readers Non-Disclosure Agreement

○ Sent
○ Beta Readers Returned Non-Disclosure Agreement

Send Round 1 Beta Readers Questionnaire

○ Sent

Send Round 1 ARC to Beta Readers

○ Sent

Edit Manuscript to Accommodate Beta Reader's Input

○ Complete

Send Round 2 Beta Readers Non-Disclosure Agreement

○ Sent
○ Beta Readers Returned Non-Disclosure Agreement

Send Round 2 Beta Readers Questionnaire

○ Sent

☐ **Send Round 2 ARC to Beta Readers**

○ Sent

☐ **Edit Manuscript to Accommodate Beta Reader's Input**

○ Complete

☐ **Send Round 3 Beta Readers Non-Disclosure Agreement**

○ Sent
○ Beta Readers Returned Non-Disclosure Agreement

☐ **Send Round 3 Beta Readers Questionnaire**

○ Sent

☐ **Send Round 3 ARC to Beta Readers**

○ Sent

☐ **Edit Manuscript to Accommodate Beta Reader's Input**

○ Complete

☐ **Send Round 4 Beta Readers Non-Disclosure Agreement**

○ Sent
○ Beta Readers Returned Non-Disclosure Agreement

☐ **Send Round 4 Beta Readers Questionnaire**

○ Sent

Send Round 4 ARC to Beta Readers

○ Sent

Edit Manuscript to Accommodate Beta Reader's Input

○ Complete
○ Send Manuscript to Copy Editor

NOTES

BETA READER TRACKING LOG

NOTE: Use this form to track your Beta Reader Process

BETA READER NAME	NDA SENT	NDA SIGNED	ARC SENT	FEEDBACK RETURNED

Check Out Author Resources

○ Completed

4. THREE MONTHS BEFORE LAUNCH

Right at three months before I launch a book my nerves start to hover inside me thinking of everything I must accomplish between now and launch day. The first thing to do is set up your Amazon account if you don't already have one and go to KDP.com. This is the Kindle Direct Publishing site where you should add your book and start the pre-order process.

There are several things you need to know when adding your book; you must choose your keywords and your categories. Both these have a direct impact on your book's Amazon rankings. If you use the wrong keywords or list your book in an inadequate category, you lose your potential in rankings. That is why it is essential to do both a keyword search and category search before selecting them.

Keyword Search Optimization

To search for keywords that best fit your book and genre, I use this keyword tool: https://keywordtool.io/amazon which is free and extremely easy to use.

Primarily you can search for your book's topic, and it provides the keywords most used. For my novel *Never Stop Running*, I typed my topic, "reincarnation" into the search bar and received more than fifty suggested keywords. The goal is to choose those that rank the highest in your search because those are the ones that readers have consistently searched.

Keyword Tool

Find Great Keywords Using Amazon Autocomplete

Google   YouTube   Bing   **Amazon**   eBay   App Store   Instagram   Twitter

| All ▾ | Reincarnation | | United States / English | ▾ |

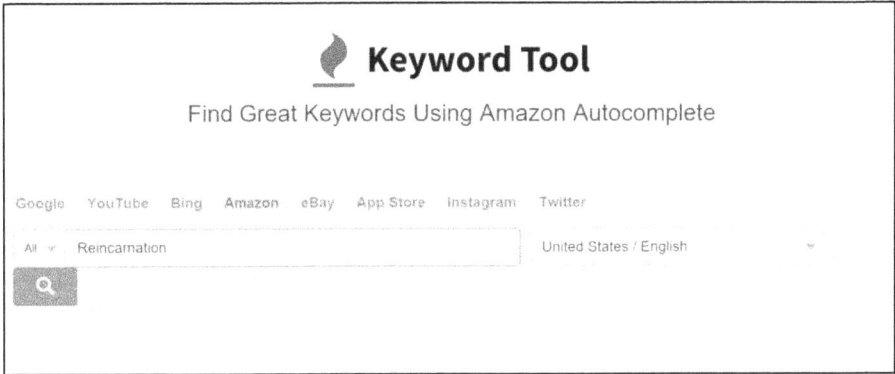

Once I clicked on the red search tab, I received the following results.

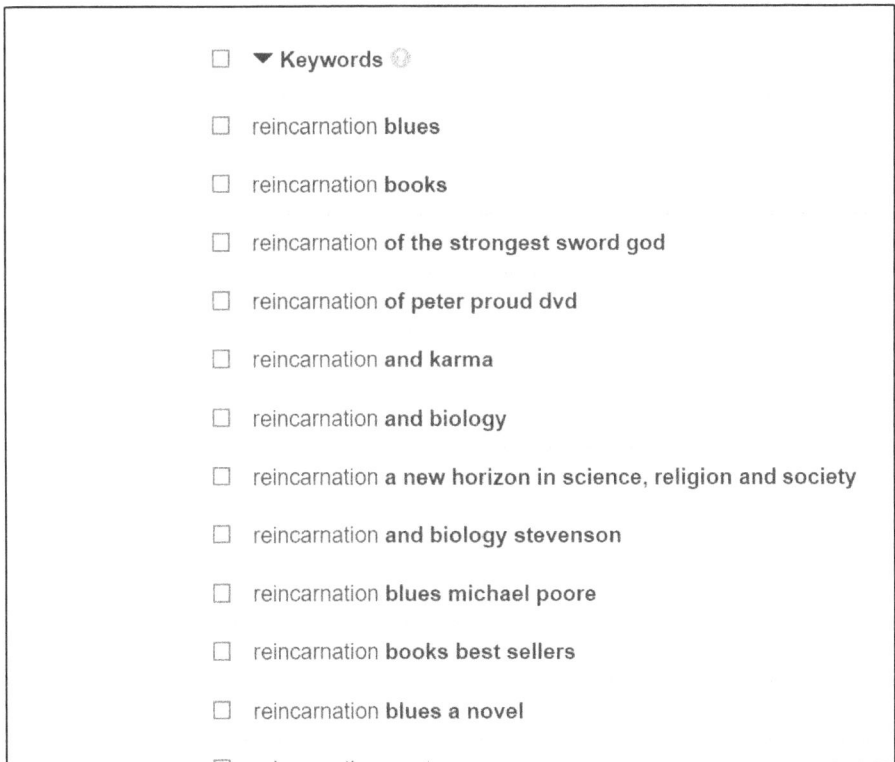

☐   ▼ Keywords ⟳

☐   reincarnation **blues**

☐   reincarnation **books**

☐   reincarnation **of the strongest sword god**

☐   reincarnation **of peter proud dvd**

☐   reincarnation **and karma**

☐   reincarnation **and biology**

☐   reincarnation **a new horizon in science, religion and society**

☐   reincarnation **and biology stevenson**

☐   reincarnation **blues michael poore**

☐   reincarnation **books best sellers**

☐   reincarnation **blues a novel**

… and so forth. The results provided the most used keywords; therefore, when I created the book title in my KDP bookshelf, I choose seven of the ones I felt made the most sense, those being:

Another feature of the Keyword Tool is that you can also identify the best hashtags for your book across multiple platforms such as Google, YouTube, and Instagram. When you post on social media, hashtags serve to help people find your posts about specific topics. When I entered "serial killer book" in the Keyword Tool, it identified forty-nine hashtags for *The Keystroke Killer: Transcendence*, such as those in the picture below.

and, so forth.

Setting Categories

Choosing your Kindle categories or book categories will have a direct impact on whether you become a #1 New Release or bestseller on Amazon. You won't become a bestseller if you choose the wrong one. You have a great deal at stake in finding the perfect category. Here is a secret that Amazon doesn't publicize – you can have seven categories, but you must know the inside method. I'll walk you through that in the next section too.

The Nitty-Gritty of Categories

The first consideration in choosing a category is to research the categories available on Amazon. Search for books in your genre and style and find the top-selling books and write their categories down. When I typed in "Reincarnation Books," the most popular book popped to the top. I scrolled down to look at their Amazon ranking.

Amazon Best Sellers Rank: #474,799 in Books (See Top 100 in Books)
    #673 in Books > Literature & Fiction > History & Criticism > Movements & Periods > **Renaissance**
    #8559 in Books > Romance > **Fantasy**
    #9434 in Books > Science Fiction & Fantasy > Fantasy > **Romantic**

Wow! Four hundred seventy-four thousand seven hundred ninety-nine books and this book is rated at #673. Who wants to compete with that? Do you know how many books I would have to sell to get close? I must sell one hundred books to get close. So, move on. Look for another book down the list until you find one where there isn't that much competition.

Amazon Best Sellers Rank: #360,096 in Books (See Top 100 in Books)
    #468 in Books > Religion & Spirituality > New Age & Spirituality > **Reincarnation**

This one is better, but not perfect. Keep searching through the books until you locate the lowest competition book in the Top 100 in books.

However, I would only have to sell less than twenty books to get into the top.

Amazon Best Sellers Rank: #34,620 in Books (See Top 100 in Books)
#37 in Books > Religion & Spirituality > Occult & Paranormal > Parapsychology > **Near-Death Experiences**
#52 in Books > Religion & Spirituality > Religious Studies > **Science & Religion**
#74 in Books > Christian Books & Bibles > Theology > **Eschatology**

Now we're talking. If I chose the lower ranking categories for *Never Stop Running*, I would be competing in that category with less than thirty-five thousand books, rather than a half-million books. Search wisely when choosing the categories.

When you first use KDP to publish your book, you're only allowed to set two categories. I've bet you seen books on Amazon with seven or more categories. How did they do that? The process is rather simple – call Amazon KDP once your book is published and has been assigned the ASIN number. You won't be able to do it until then.

The picture below shows A.D.A.M. is the pre-order state and The *Keystroke Killer: Transcendence* in the published state. Notice under the pricing that A.D.A.M. doesn't have the ASIN number.

The second method involves emailing them. To do that go to your Author Central Page, click on the Help Tab, and compose an email that includes the specific categories you want to be added. Go to the Contact Us page and identify why you are contacting them. Choose the following answers to obtain the best results.

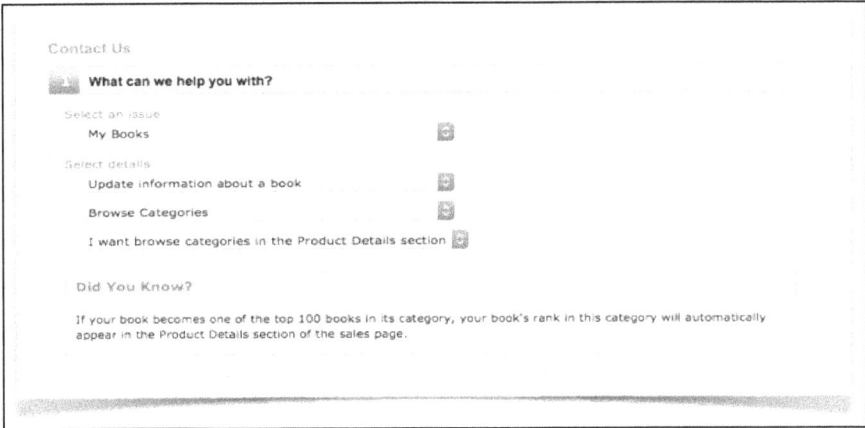

Now draft the email which must include:

- Author's Name
- Title of the Book
- Your ASIN Number

For example:

To: Customer Service

I am author Dr. Melissa Caudle, and I'd like my book The Keystroke Killer: Transcendence (ASIN – 1718872569) in the following categories.

- *> Mystery, Thriller & Suspense > Thrillers & Suspense > Supernatural > Serial Killers*
- *> Mystery, Thriller & Suspense > Thrillers & Suspense > Crime & Mystery*

Thank you in advance for your attention to my request.

Best Regards,
Dr. Melissa Caudle
Author

Launch Pre-Orders

With your keywords and categories set you're ready to launch your book. Please go through the set-up process on KDP. You set the date, but your manuscript doesn't have to be polished at this stage. Amazon will provide you with a cutoff date that your final manuscript must be completed.

Once I do this, I also order a proof paperback copy of my book so that I can read and edit it, as well as to make sure the cover is exactly how I want it. Then, I blast my pre-order availability on social media sites.

Press Kit

At this stage, I must continue to make changes to my manuscript based on the input from my beta readers and schedule my book tours. However, there is more to go as I must also concentrate on putting together my PDF press kit and printed press kit. Press kits help you to market your book to journalists, bookstores, libraries, and book clubs who ask you to speak. Here is a list of what goes in your PDF press kit:

- Your Press Release
- Your Sell Sheet
- Your Bio
- An Excerpt
- A PDF Business Card

Your printed press kit will be identical except you want to either bind it or put it in a folder. Upon delivering it include your business card and a bookmark. After my book launched, if I sent or hand delivered a press kit, I also added my book. In fact, your book is your best business card. A national television producer interviewed me for a show, and I sent her review copies of all my books. They sit on the edge of her desk. Why she keeps them there, I do not know, but I owe her a huge favor because her colleagues see them. She told me they always ask about them, and then they end up buying them. I have had several who called me and ordered an autographed copy.

SCHEDULE APPEARANCES AND INTERVIEWS

Now is the time to reach out to the presidents and members of book clubs and schedule an appearance or a book reading. Do the same thing with bookstores, coffee shops, and libraries. Another avenue is to let schools know that you're available for career days.

Speaking at a career day to a bunch of students may not sound like you're going to sell many books to the children, but that isn't your target audience. Those teachers and parents are. When I speak at schools on career day, I always bring bookmarks for the students and the entire faculty and staff. I leave them in the teacher lounge and ask the principal if I can put them in the teacher's mailboxes. Students take the bookmarks home; their parents see them and ask. Bingo! Marketing right out of the mouths of babes.

One of my many styles of bookmarks.

Interviews are golden. Make it a point to reach out and obtain as many meetings as you can in all forms of media including radio, television, podcasts, and on blogs. Each time you speak or are interviewed I advise for you to issue a press release about it and blast it on your social media sites. This isn't the time to be shy.

One thing about doing podcast and radio interviews is that you want to provide quality sound free of excess outside and inside noise. I solved that problem by purchasing a USB quality microphone, and a portable sound booth and a pop filter. My radio and podcast interviews are clear and don't make me sound like I am in a tunnel.

Pictured above is the actual booth isolation shield I use. I also purchased a pop filter and a shock mount on Amazon. I must add that my microphone is an Audio-Technica AT2020USB+ Cardioid Condenser USB Microphone in white. It works flawlessly.

Notice I have it placed on a TV stand over a very thick blanket which also helps the noise.

Written interviews are also important. My publisher, Absolute Author Publishing House, provides free written author interviews at:

www.absoluteauthor.com

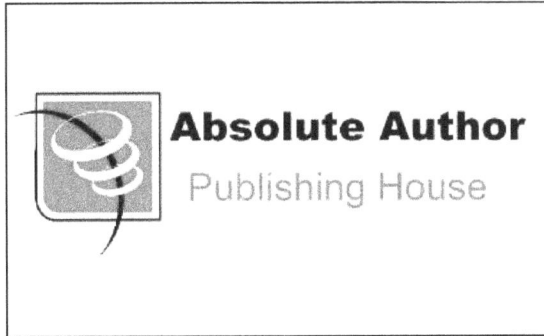

One-A-Day Posts

Do you remember that arsenal of graphic mock-up images I told you to create for your marketing tools? It is now time to splatter them on your social media sites. I have one hundred images made so each day until launch I post a different one on my social media sites.

Add Quote Cards to Your Arsenal

Quote cards use the same graphics I mentioned for the mock-up ads, except you use quotes from the book or your reviewers. Please make sure you ask your reviewers in advance if you can use their quotes. It is common courtesy and professionalism.

When you post them on your social media sites be sure to add a pre-order link with them. The one below is a quote card for A.D.A.M. from three of my beta readers.

"One of the most amazing novels I have ever read since *The Shape of Water*. It really put me in the moment and captivated my attention. I couldn't put it down" Erin W.

"A must-read page-turning novel that will have you grab you. It made me wonder what else could be out there?" Kelly C

"If your looking for a love story, don't buy this. This is science fiction at its best. Don't pass this one up." Frank G.

Pre-order today on Amazon

A Novel by Dr. Melissa Caudle

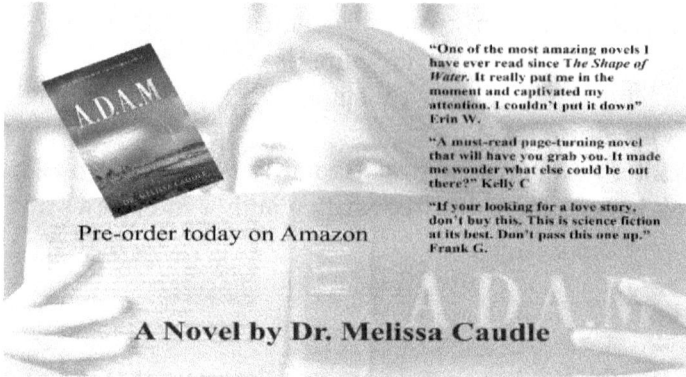

Giveaways and Advanced Review Copies

One way to generate early reviews on your social media sites is by creating a giveaway of an advance reader copy. This helps to create a buzz about your book. The best things I love about giveaways are the low-cost factor for an author, and the excellent momentum it provides for your book. I'm sure you have seen them on blogs, Amazon, and Goodreads. You must carefully plan your giveaway and make it fair, or readers will not participate.

Use the following guidelines to plan a successful giveaway of your Advanced Review Copy (ARC).

Decide on a Giveaway Date

As silly as this may sound the date you choose to start your giveaway contest is essential. Authors make a mistake and think that Saturdays are the best day of the week. I'm here to tell you weekends are the worst possible days of the week for a launch. People are generally busy and away from their computers. However, Mondays for me are the best dates because historically my blog gets the most views and new hits on Monday morning. I reason that this is because they are back at their desks and I schedule my blog release or newsletter to arrive in their mailboxes at 6:00 a.m. The next best day is Tuesday. I advise you to look at your blog stats or if you plan on posting your giveaway on someone else's blog, inquire about the day of the week they receive the most views.

Develop the Rules for the Contest

You must carefully design your rules and publish them for everyone to see. Your rule or rules can be as simple as: "Enter today for your chance for an advance copy of my new novel. Leave a comment on my blog by Sunday 9:00 p.m. CST to enter. One person will be randomly selected using Random.org. For your entry to be valid, you must leave your e-mail address with your comment. Please note that paperback books can only be sent to a street address in the United States and Canada. If you are the winner outside of these two countries, you will receive a PDF file. The winner will be announced on my blog on May 24, 2019."

I also allow extra entries as a bonus by adding: "If you subscribe to my blog you will be entered twice, and if you are already a blog subscriber, you are already entered."

Publicize the Giveaway

Once again it would be best if you marketed your giveaway contest. Use the same mock-up images of your covers and add the graphics as necessary. Post those on all your social media sites and blast it on your blog and in your newsletter. Reach out to other bloggers and ask if they will announce the giveaway too. I know as a blogger I love to do that for people because it brings more readers to my site from different authors.

How to Enter

Leave a comment on my blog by January 16, 2019, 9:00 p.m. CST for your chance to win your advance copy of *Never Stop Running*. For an extra entry, subscribe to my blog. If you are already a subscriber you have been automatically entered. Ten winners will be chosen by Random.com and announced January 21, 2019 in my blog.

Good Luck!

www.drmelcaudle.blogspot.com

About Random.org

Random.org randomly generates numbers to determine your giveaway winner. To use it effectively use it, number every subscriber. Do the same thing for every comment. Then let Random.org do the rest. When the random number is chosen, you have your winner. Notify them and follow through by sending them the ARC.

Three additional sites can run your entire giveaways for you:

- Rafflecopter
- Instafreebie
- Amazon

Check them out.

HOW TO LAUNCH AND MARKET A BOOK

Announce the winner

Announcing the winner is so much fun for me; I always send them a personal email to inform them that they have won and to obtain their postal address. I usually get an email within the hour. After I have their confirmation, I post the winner all over my social media sites and release a press release which also creates a buzz in the marketplace.

Plan a Launch Party

Long before your book launches you must plan the launch party. You have time now, but you won't later. I hear you. First, I told you that you had to treat your writing as a business, then I said you had to become a marketer, and now I'm saying you are now a party planner. Unless you're rich and you can afford for someone else to plan it, you can't turn over this duty. So, here are the steps to planning a successful launch party.

Decide on a Location

It is all about location, location, and location. My first launch parties are usually in my hometown and close to home so I can invite my friends and family. I choose my site to accommodate the theme of my book if possible. Mostly, I prefer a local restaurant with a large bar and a private room. That way the catering is easier to handle. I contact the manager and book the date.

The beautiful part of using my local bar is I'm not charged for the venue. I do not purchase alcohol, but I do pay for tea, coffee, water, and soft drinks and appetizers for the crowd. The bar benefits because they get an influx of new people who spend money on cocktails. They provide me with a table for my book displays, my raffle jar, and a place at the bar for me to autograph my books. It's a fun place to mingle, and I don't have clean-up chores.

Another bonus is that I always get new fans who are dining at the restaurant or who came to the bar. They join in on the fun, and I usually sell twenty books that way.

Ask for Help

Ask friends and family to help you organize and support during the party. Let them volunteer for their 'duties.' The duties I usually need are:

- A Greeter

- A photographer and a videographer

- Someone who will take orders and sell books

- Someone in charge of signing up people to my blog

- A raffle person
- If you're not having your launch party in a venue or with catering, you will need someone in charge of refreshments. It could be as simple as popcorn and soda or elaborate to a buffet or potluck.

Send Out Invitations

Use your social media platforms to send out invitations and announcements for the launch party. I strongly suggest for your family members, your editors, and beta readers you use snail mail with invitations because they deserve the golden treatment.

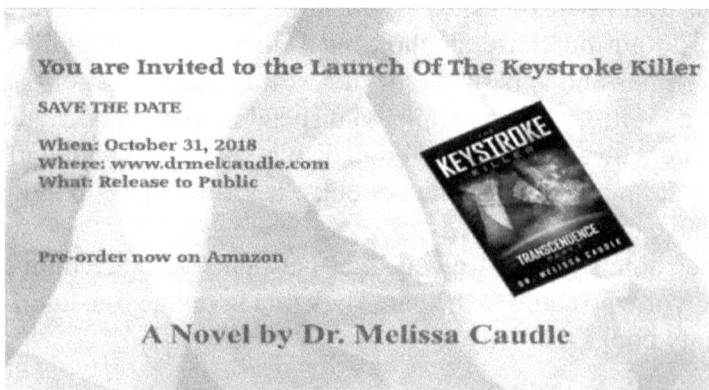

You are Invited to the Launch Of The Keystroke Killer

SAVE THE DATE

When: October 31, 2018
Where: www.drmelcaudle.com
What: Release to Public

Pre-order now on Amazon

A Novel by Dr. Melissa Caudle

HOW TO LAUNCH AND MARKET A BOOK

Market Your Party

Do I need to advise you to market your party? Blast it everywhere and encourage your launch team to distribute it to their social media sites as well.

During the Party

It is a must to identify your branding presence during your launch party. The two best ways are to have a two by three-foot poster made of your book and place it on the table where you will sell your books and a two by the eight-foot banner. I use a local logo printing company for mine, but there are plenty of alternatives on the Internet.

During the party have your guests register for door prizes. I also make sure everyone goes home with a bookmark and my business card. It should go without saying to sell your books -- not only the book that you just launched but also any previous novels. Be sure to offer free autographs.

Other touches are to hold a reading of an excerpt and to show your book's trailers on the televisions if the venue allows.

Make certain that you do not let people monopolize your time. Everyone who attends needs to speak with you, and you need to engage in conversation with them. This is not the time to say, "Hey, please buy my book." Rather talk about them. Thank them for coming. Be personable. Your books will sell themselves at the launch party.

AUTHOR

Dr. Melissa Caudle

The Keystroke Killer

Never Stop Running

A.D.A.M.

10.31.2018

The After Party

I got this idea of an after party working in the film industry. After Parties are a fantastic way to say thank you to those who helped you before and during the party. Take them to eat or to another bar and treat them like royalty. They deserve it.

The Day After the Launch Party

Blast pictures and videos on your social media and write an original blog post showing all the fun you had. Last, but not least, thank your team publicly in your blog or social media post.

THREE MONTHS BEFORE LAUNCH CHECKLIST

Categories, Press Kit, and Launch Party

Keyword Search

○ Search Optimization on Keyword Tool Completed

List Keywords:

1. _____
2. _____
3. _____
4. _____
5. _____

○ Search for Hashtags on Keyword Tool Completed

List Hashtags:

1. _____
2. _____
3. _____
4. _____
5. _____

Identify Categories

○ Categories Completed

List Categories.

1. _____
2. _____
3. _____
4. _____
5. _____

Upload Manuscript and Cover to KDP

○ Publish for Pre-Orders
○ Market Pre-Order Availability

Develop Press Kit

○ Press Releases to Announce Pre-Orders Sent
○ Sell Sheet
○ Bio
○ Excerpt
○ Updated and Posted to Website

Schedule Radio/TV Interviews

○ Completed
Date:
Time:
Location:

Date:
Time:

Location:

Date:
Time:
Location:

One-A-Day Posts

- Day 1
- Day 2
- Day 3
- Day 4
- Day 5
- Day 6
- Day 7
- Day 8
- Day 9
- Day 10
- Day 11
- Day 12
- Day 13
- Day 14
- Day 15
- Day 16
- Day 17
- Day 18
- Day 19
- Day 20
- Day 21
- Day 22
- Day 23
- Day 24
- Day 25
- Day 26
- Day 27
- Day 28
- Day 29
- Day 30

Create Quote Ad Cards

- Completed

Send Our ARC's

Start Giveaway Contest

- Set Giveaway Date
- Develop Rules for Giveaway Contest
- Publicize Giveaways
- Select and Announce Winner

○ Send Prizes to Winner

Plan Launch Party

○ Set Date

Location is: _____

○ Send Out Invitations
○ Identify Helpers

List Your Helpers

    1. _____

    2. _____

    3. _____

    4. _____

    5. _____

○ Market Party

○ After Party Location is: _____

○ Blast Pictures of After Party

○ Send Thank-You Notes

○ Follow Up on Orders

NOTES

5. TWO MONTHS BEFORE LAUNCH

Two months out I call the rinse and repeat cycle because you must continue what you have already been doing to launch your book as the #1 New Release. However, it is a little easier because you have your tools already in place and at your disposal.

I'll never forget the morning of January 19, 2019. First, it was my mother's birthday – my cover model for *Never Stop Running*. I couldn't sleep the night before knowing that the novel would go public. I was a nervous wreck. I wanted the book to rise above the others only to honor my mother. I had been on a mission to author the novel, edit it, and place her photograph on the cover to fulfill her bucket list before she passed. The doctor gave her six months to live at the maximum after he diagnosed her with stage four lung cancer. Talk about pressure, that was pressure. So, to me getting this novel published and rated the #1 New Release had a different meaning for me. It wasn't about getting the recognition, nor was it about finally making a little money from my writing. It was all about honoring my mother. I did it!

I didn't know two months out from my launch date, my mother's birthday, if the book would be ready for publication. I knew I was a power-writer because on average I write or edit thirty pages a day. Then suddenly, I realized that all my planning from the previous four months worked. My book was ready to go. I waited and sat on the book for two months before publishing it so that I could release it on my mother's birthday.

During that time, I learned a valuable lesson – novels are like fine wine. The longer one ages, the better it gets. I took the next two months honing my marketing skills to ensure that the book would launch successfully. I focused on doing important marketing stuff instead of writing. Trust me, I still wrote; that's how A.D.A.M. flourished into a novel.

During the second to the last month, it is the time to get into the routine of daily marketing. I spend about two hours a day in this month marketing and the rest of the day polishing my final manuscript. Focus! Focus! Focus! This month you must concentrate your attention on the following:

- Develop your mantra or war chant – you're going to need it
- Polishing your script, if it isn't already
- Continue to post on social media your ads and trailer(s)
- Everything you've been doing on social media continues
- Schedule book signings
- Schedule blog tour
- Set up Google Alerts for your name and for your book(s)
- Start the audiobook process

Develop Your Mantra or War Chant

See! That's not so bad, is it? Compared to what you have done, it isn't. Good grief Charlie Brown, you authored a freaking novel or non-fiction book. CONGRATULATIONS! So, take in a slow deep breath at the beginning of this month and dream of the possibilities.

To make it through and provide you with a little extra boost, develop a mantra or your launch war chant. Let it inspire you. Write it on sticky notes and post them on the wall above your monitor. Place them on your bathroom mirror so you can read it when you wash your face or brush your teeth. I posted them on my refrigerator, above the toilet roll dispenser on my closet door, and my piano; any place is game.

My mantra is, "Today you will achieve the impossible because you have already done the possible." This keeps me going toward my dreams and goals. Now think about your mantra or war chant. What will inspire you?

Schedule Book Signings

Book signings after your book has launched are the cornerstone to you as an author. The hurdle you must leap is organizing your calendar to accommodate them. For your launch campaign to be successful, do not overlook the necessity of a book signing. Meeting your target audience and potential buyer face to face cannot be measured in terms of the time you spend at them. Meeting them is priceless.

Many readers want autographed copies of from their favorite author. That is one reason I sell them on my website. On a side note, after Never Stop Running launched, people requested not just my autograph, but also my mother's. I guess I marketed my cover model. We accommodated their request I'm happy to report. Those five hundred copies are priceless to me because they have my mother's signature along with mine. Trust me when I tell you I have a double-autographed copy for all my children and grandchildren. So, never underestimate the power of yours.

You won't have time to schedule your signings after the launch. It will be too late. Venues get booked, and there is no time to schedule. Do it during this month.

To identify potential bookstores to schedule a book signing, search your city's website and review the Calendar of Events. Usually, other book signings are listed as well. Bingo! That's where you call first.

You can use the same procedure for any city you desire to hold a book signing. This is where your sell sheets come in handy. Either visit the store in person with your sell sheet in your hand or call a store and ask to speak to the manager.

Have your pitch ready. It can be short and sweet like this.

"Hi, I'm Dr. Melissa Caudle, and I would love to bring customers to your bookstore by having a book signing for my new novel *Never Stop Running*."

If in person, hand them an advanced review copy and the sell sheet. If on the phone, ask if you can mail or email them information and the advanced copy. From there have a conversation and offer to help before the event.

While you are at it, ask if they would like to subscribe to your blog or email list for updates on the release or future novels. Nine times out of ten they agree. Proceed to discuss dates available and book it. If they must think about it, give them a day or two and then follow up with a phone call. Book as many signings in as many cities as you can.

Schedule Blog or Podcast Tour

Not all engagements with your readers must be in person. Blog tours are awesome. They are not expensive other than your time and the cost of advanced copies of your book. The good news is that many bloggers would rather have a digital copy to read.

Remember in earlier months when I informed you to research potential bloggers? Now that list is finally coming in handy. Half of your work is completed – you know whom to reach out to, so contact them to be a guest blogger or to be a guest on their podcasts. Likewise, if you have been participating in forums on blogs and social media, your name is already out there by now. That means, when you reach out to a blogger, they will recognize it. Now you know why I asked you to participate in social media four months ago.

From the desk of Author Melissa Caudle

I'm being interviewed by Brian Hammer Jackson
The Brian Jackson and Ellen J in the Morning Show
Join me February 11th, as I answer your questions in this 'anything goes' discussion.
10:20 a.m. CST

Brian The Hammer Jackson
INTERNET'S #1 RADIO PERSONALITY
Host of "Hammer 96.7"

KEYSTROKE
ADAM
RUNNING

There will be a giveaway!

Reach out to the bloggers and podcasters with a message and inform them that you are interested in guest blogging and in exchange, you will provide a giveaway of your book to their subscribers. Bloggers love that. You can do this with as many bloggers as you want. Here is the honey in this plan I have you developing. Remember when I informed you to write future blog posts a couple of months in advance? If you do, your blog post is pre-written. The goal as a guest blogger is to always have at least five pre-written blog posts in your arsenal. Anytime you send one as a guest blogger, write another. It takes a lot of stress off yourself.

Please don't forget about me and my blog: www.drmelcaudle.blogspot.com. I'd love to have you guest post on my blog as would my publisher at www.absoluteauthor.com. Reach out to Carol and me. You already have two blogs to schedule for your tour.

Set up a Google Alert for Your Name and Book Title(s)

Have you ever heard of Google Alerts? If you haven't, this is a tracking system which once set up will alert you each time anything about your book or your name is posted. You receive an email with the links. You want to do this so that you can find your press releases, blogs you've posted or in case any reader makes a comment about your book or leaves a review. It will save you tons of time in keeping your website updated.

How to Set up or Create a Google Alert

Sign in to https://google.com/alerts. You will need your Google ID and password. If you don't have one, you must create one. Follow the directions and prompts that they give you.

Once you are logged in, you will see a screen with some topics, but you will use the Search Option to create an alert - type in the name of your book. If you have more than one book, create an alert for each one and your name.

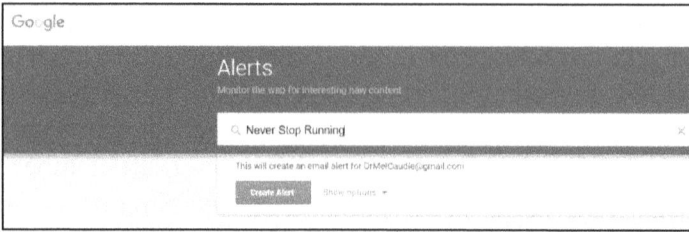

Find the Show options tab and click on it. This allows you to customize your options for the alert. Check the following areas:

- How Often – click As-it-happens
- Sources – click all options
- Language – English – if you want to add another language, you'll have to create another alert.
- Region – I choose Any Region.
- How Many – I choose the best results
- Deliver to – I have them sent to my email address; however, you can always create another email address and send them there and only use that address for the alerts.

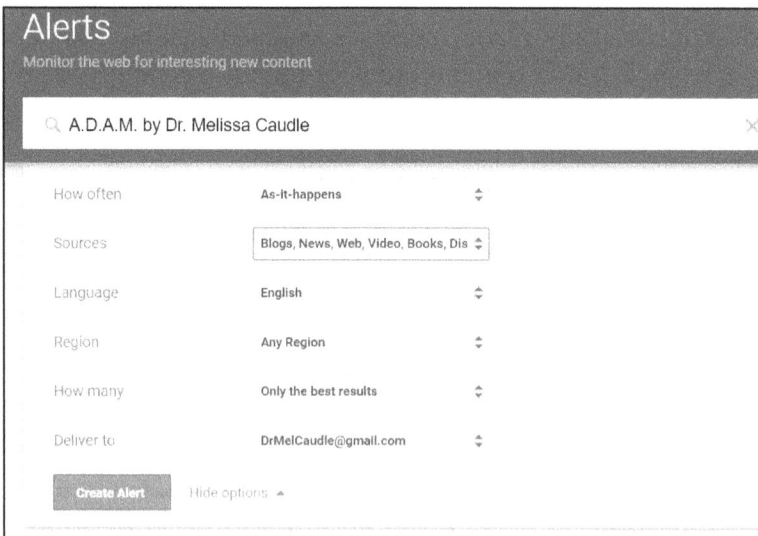

After making your selections, click on the Create Alert in the blue box and you're done. You can always change your options by clicking on the Pencil Icon, and you can eliminate them by clicking on the Trash Icon. Now you're all set to go.

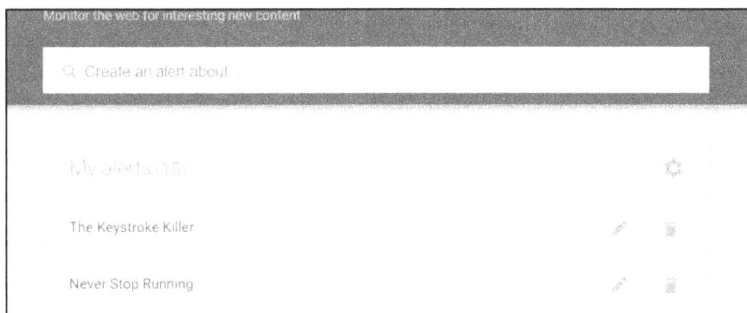

How to get Google Alerts to a Non-Google Email Address

Some writers don't have Gmail, but you can still get Google alerts on your current Yahoo, Hotmail, etc. addresses. Again, you can always create a Gmail account only to track your alerts. Since we're on the subject of Google Alerts, it's time to put it into action and copy all the links to your website to create backlinks. You can find mine on my press page.

AUDIOBOOKS

The Wall Street Journal reported that audiobooks are the fastest growing market in the book publishing world. Audible books or audiobooks are trendy in the market for a novelist. It is almost a must for an author to remain competitive in the market. So, move over E-books and paperbacks, the audiobook is taking over.

Research has shown that audiobooks are the fastest growing market for authors, so it's time to get on board. As frustrating and challenging as it may sound, it is easier than you might think. According to *The Wall Street Journal*, audiobooks are a $2.5 billion industry, and it is growing. Why? They are convenient and readers who commute listen to their books not read them. It's easy on the eyes in a world where the computer screen and our cell phones are a huge part of our culture.

If you want to expand your reader base, one of the quickest ways is to turn your novel into an audiobook. In this blog, I'm addressing the ins and outs for authors, and the variety of ways to get your novel converted into an audible book format. Are you ready?

Why are Audiobooks Growing?

There are a variety of reasons for the growth of audiobooks. Consider these:

1. Readers are always on the go using various modes of transportation:

   - Walking
   - Jogging
   - Running
   - Cars
   - Planes
   - Trains
   - Subways
   - Spaceflights (Okay, only a few, but astronauts listen to them)

2. Although audiobooks have been around for some time, readers want them more today than ever. That means you need to convert your novel to meet the supply and demand.

3. It may be difficult for you to comprehend, but some people love books who cannot read. Audiobooks make it easy for a blind person to get involved or a person who is not in the position to read for themselves. I remember when I was so sick in the hospital, I couldn't hold my head up, couldn't watch television because of my blurred vision, but I could listen to a compelling story in audiobook form.

Why Should You Convert Your Book into an Audiobook?

There is less competition for audiobooks than there are for paperbacks and E-Books. That means the potential for your earning power increases and audiobooks never sell out. Also, the process is probably more straightforward than you imagine with a variety of services at your disposal.

The Process of Creating an Audiobook

There are a couple of ways:

- Have it produced, hire a voiceover narrator and the final narrator?
- Produce it yourself, hire the voiceover narrator and go to a recording studio
- Produce it yourself, purchase the equipment and narrate it yourself
- Alternatively, a combination of the above

Do You Do-it-Yourself or Hire it Out?

There are pros and cons to both methods to produce an audiobook. Of course, if you hire to have it done by a professional narrator, you will have a professional product to sell. The fees to have an audiobook produced range in cost depending on your area and could rise above $1,000 or more depending on the experience of the narrator. I chose to hire a professional, so I saved my money until I had enough. Ouch! However, you can do it yourself with the right equipment.

The Basic Equipment

If you choose to produce it yourself, you will have to purchase the equipment for quality control, audition the narrator and become responsible for editing the final product. Wow! Before you get off this gravy train, it's not as expensive as you might think. Let me explain.

To produce your audiobook yourself, you will need quality equipment. You probably have a computer which is the most significant expense. Here are the items you will need:

- A desktop computer, the newer, the better
- A quality XLR microphone
- A pop filter to cover the microphone
- A stand, preferably one that attaches to your desk
- A USB2 multimixer that connects my XLR mic to the USB port on your computer
- A quiet place to record with carpet to prevent noise bounce from the floor
- Audacity - A free software program to record and edit your files.

Now you might be thinking that sounds like a lot of money. Not really, one of my authors bought her entire equipment on Amazon as a complete package for less than $100. Your goal is to research the equipment and find what you need.

Here is the package she bought from Amazon. No, I don't get any money for promoting these packages; they are just examples.

Aokeo AK-70 Professional Studio Live Stream Broadcasting Recording Condenser Microphone With AK-35 Suspension Scissor Arm Stand, Shock Mount, Pop Filter, USB Sound Card and Mounting Clamp. This complete system was under $80 shipped in less than three days to your home. You will also need the pop filter which costs less than $10. Now a word on sound quality.

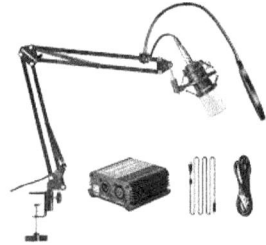

ACX.Com

I chose to hire it out and used ACX.com. ACX is awesome. In one place you can audition your narrators, produce your audiobook, and publish it which links your books on Amazon. Here is the screenshot for the audition page for *Never Stop Running*.

When you study the image, you can see that I have one audiobook that is currently open for auditions, I have two books in production, and I have twenty-two new auditions. At the time of this writing, I was in the middle of the audition process. The process is simple, you add your book's title, ISBN, and off you go. There is a place for you to submit your script for the audition so the narrators can download it. Before you publish your book, you can hire a narrator to do an excerpt of the book or one chapter and post it on your website and blog. To increase subscribers and to an email list, offer it for free if they subscribe.

TWO MONTHS BEFORE LAUNCH CHECKLIST

Book Tours, Google Alerts, Pod Casts, and Audiobook

Develop Your Mantra

○ Write Mantra
○ Post Mantra Around the House

Schedule Book Signings

○ Completed
Date:
Time:
Location:

Date:
Time:
Location:

Date:
Time:
Location:

Schedule Blog Tour

○ Completed
Date:
Time:
Location:

Date:
Time:
Location:

Schedule Pod Cast Tour

○ Completed
Date:
Time:
Location:

Date:
Time:
Location:

Date:
Time:
Location:

Set Up Google Alerts

○ One for Your Name
○ One for Each Book Title

Begin Audio Book Process

○ Join ACX
○ Post Audition Script
○ Listen to Auditions
○ Hire Audio Narrator
○ Approve First Fifteen Minutes
○ Approve Final Audiobook

6. ONE MONTH BEFORE LAUNCH

One month before your book's launch you need to go full force on your marketing activities. Do it for thirty minutes three times a day. I suggest early in the morning, mid-afternoon, and one around 8:00 p.m. The reason is that individuals get on their social media sites at various times of the day. If you only post once, that post is likely to get buried. That is why it is important to post at different intervals for the most target specific posts. Each time, post to your media sites that the countdown to launch day has begun.

Countdown Ads – One a Day

Now is the time to use the mock-up ads you created and post them to all social media sites. This time you will add the countdown number of days until launch at the top of thirty different ads you have already established. For example:

"30 Days till Launch"
"29 Days till Launch"
"28 Days till Launch"

Continue the countdown ads all the way until you launch your book. When you use a different graphic each time, it keeps it fresh to the eyes of a potential reader. The consistency factor is in your book's cover that now is recognizable. Another bit of advice is to push your ads on Facebook, Goodreads, Amazon, and Bookbub. Weigh the cost factor and do your research targeting where your audience hangs out.

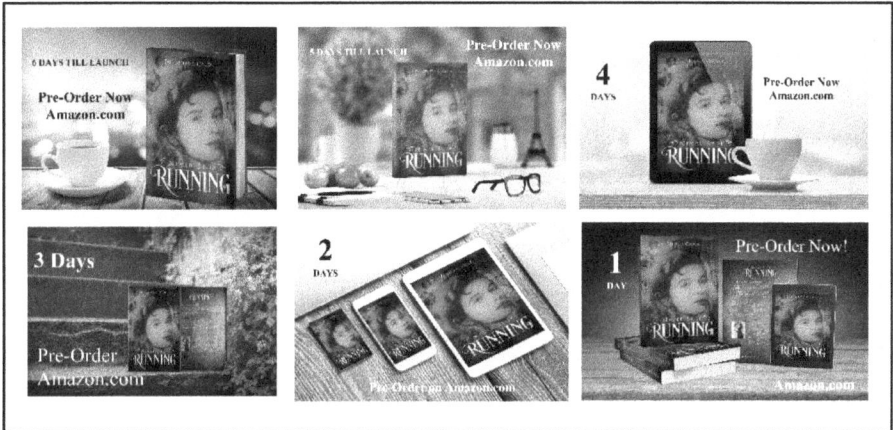

Create a Pinterest Board Featuring Your Book

Over the course of the last five months, you should have created lots of ads and gathered multiple images. Use them to your marketing advantage and create a Pinterest Board that is only about your book. Finally, everything will be in one place. Once completed, promote your Pinterest board.

Repost and Reshare

To add to your book's buzz, you can repost or reshare prior posts. It takes a bit of time, but the rewards will be worth it. Also, when it comes to reposting on Facebook, always click the feature to save the post. That way when you need to share the information again, you don't have to recreate the wheel so to speak.

Post a Teaser on Wattpad

Wattpad.com is a website to share your writing and gain a fan base. Use it to share short stories or post an excerpt or the first chapters of your book on it to increase sales. If they like what they read, they'll go to the link you provide and purchase it.

These posts are perfect on your website and your social media sites.

Once a Week Send a Reminder Email to Your Subscribers

You don't want to overburden the readers who subscribed to your email list, so every Monday, author an email about the launch. Give them excerpts to read from the book right in their email and the link to pre-purchase your book. Also, if you have an excerpt from your audiobook, send that to them as well.

Post Beta Reader's Reviews

Your beta readers are the perfect people to write early reviews of your novel. Contact them and ask them for quotes or to write reviews that you can use on your website, quote cards, and for the flipbook trailer. They can be short and sweet like the examples below which some of my readers left for me for my novel A.D.A.M.

> *"A heartfelt emotional story."* Ann D.
> *"All the Hallmarks of a bestseller."* Mary S.
> *"Engaging and fast-paced. The must-read of the year."* Tom M.
> *"Brilliantly Plotted. Beautifully written."* Erin W.
> *"Moving and Gripping."* Tina R.
> *"Gut-wrenching at its best. I couldn't put it down."* Charles F.

Create an Amazon Affiliate Program

You can earn money on your website or blog when you sell your books through the Amazon Affiliate Program. It won't make you rich, but you do make more money from the sale of your book because of the advertising link. When an individual purchases your book from your affiliate link, at the end of the month, you receive commission in addition to your standard royalty. I make about twenty-five cents more a book over my usual royalty when someone purchases it using my affiliate link. Again, that may not seem like much, but it only takes four quarters to make a dollar and when you sell one thousand copies of your book from an amazon link that is two hundred and fifty dollars I wouldn't have earned. Therefore, don't discount this option to increase your earnings.

Once you register, Amazon will assign you a unique associate's identification; mine is "DrMelsMarket-20." From there you can research specific links to your novel with your associate's identification embedded into the link. I use these links to advertise my novels on my website, blog, and social media sites. Always use these links for your promotions, pre-sales, and sales.

If you blog and recommend items as I do, such as art graphic design software, publishing software, or items like microphones and audio equipment for book narrators which makes an author's journey more manageable, generate links for those as well. When someone clicks on a link, you earn a commission for those in the affiliate program. A bonus earning potential is that for the next twenty-four hours if they purchase anything on Amazon, you receive a commission for those purchased items too. It doesn't amount to much, but a little money is better than not making any. Over the course of the last six months, I have earned nearly five hundred dollars this way. Please keep in mind that your earning potential will vary from mine because I have more than 125,000 subscribers to my blog and average about one thousand new hits a day. So, it will take time to build up your audience. To sign up to the Amazon Affiliate Program go to this link:

https://affiliate-program.amazon.com

Once you are signed up, you can search for any novel or item and receive the URL link for it. Here is the beautiful part, you can opt to have the URL in a long link, a shortened link or in HTML which will embed the picture of the item and the link to purchase it. Refer to the samples below for my book A.D.A.M.

The first thing you will have to do is to locate your book's link by either the ASIN number or title. If you are searching for a product, you will need the specific title.

From here, type in the search bar the item or book you want to establish an affiliate link.

Press "Go," and the results will come up.

Now press "Get Link" and you will be taken to a screen that will ask you the type of link that you desire. At this point, you can decide whether you want a link for the text and image, text only, or image only. The picture below is for the text and image. If you only want the text, click on the "Text Only" area and for the image only click on that area.

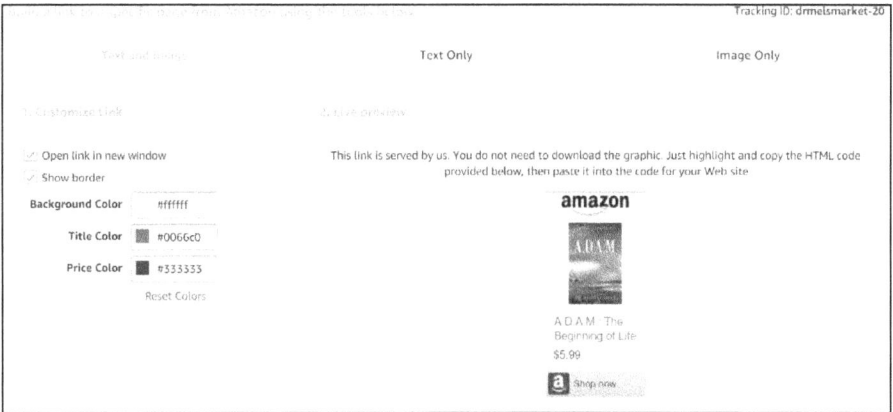

Once I decide on the type of link, I click on it. In the example below I only wanted the text, and I wanted the shortened link.

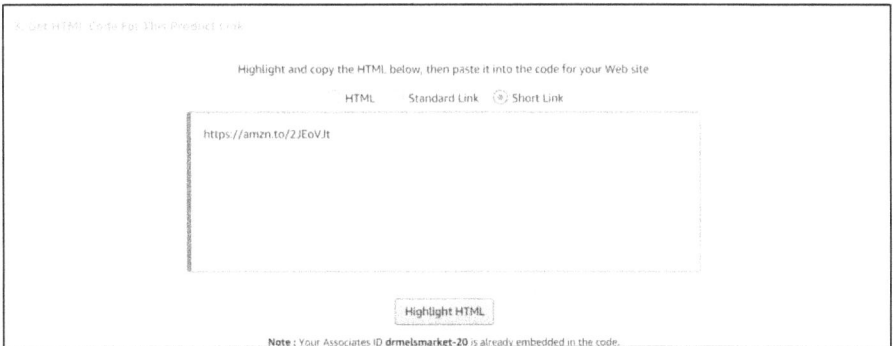

The only thing left is for me to copy and paste it into the area that I want it to embed in my blog or to a Facebook post providing a link to purchase my book.

ONE MONTH BEFORE LAUNCH CHECKLIST

The Final Countdown

Create a Pinterest Board for Your Book

○ Completed

One-A-Day Post
Post a countdown to launch ad on social media for each of the next thirty days.

○ Day 1
○ Day 2
○ Day 3
○ Day 4
○ Day 5
○ Day 6
○ Day 7
○ Day 8
○ Day 9
○ Day 10
○ Day 11
○ Day 12
○ Day 13
○ Day 14
○ Day 15
○ Day 16
○ Day 17
○ Day 18
○ Day 19
○ Day 20

○ Day 21
○ Day 22
○ Day 23
○ Day 24
○ Day 25
○ Day 26
○ Day 27
○ Day 28
○ Day 29
○ Day 30

NOTES

Post New Teaser Trailer

- ○ WattPad
- ○ Social Media Sites
- ○ Vimeo
- ○ YouTube

Blog Weekly to Remind Book Launch

- ○ Week 1
- ○ Week 2
- ○ Week 3
- ○ Week 4

Post Beta Reader's Reviews

- ○ Post on Website
- ○ Update Review Ad Cards
- ○ Post on Social Media
- ○ Issue Press Release

Create an Amazon Affiliate Program

- ○ Completed

NOTES

7. LAUNCH DAY

Congratulations! You made it to one of the most critical milestones in your life. You are a published author. Now the Debbie Downer – you'll never be finished marketing if you want to increase your sales. The first thing I do on launch day is to go to Amazon and look up my book to see if I published as the #1 New Release. It's a great feeling to see that orange banner by your listing price. Then I check it before I go to bed to make sure I saw it. It is an overwhelming feeling.

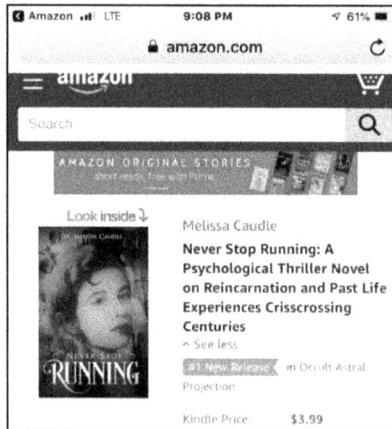

Social Media Posts

Post everywhere you can that today your book has launched and include the Amazon affiliate access link where they can buy it. Share pictures celebrating your book's launch and ask for people to share their photo holding your book.

Update Your Social Media Banners

Now that your book has launched, update your Facebook banner to show your new book. Keep your branding but give it a fresh look. I changed my banner the moment I announced the pre-order for A.D.A.M. to include all three of my novels. For my profile picture, I use one of me being interviewed holding three of my non-fiction books. Success! I have showcased six of my books.

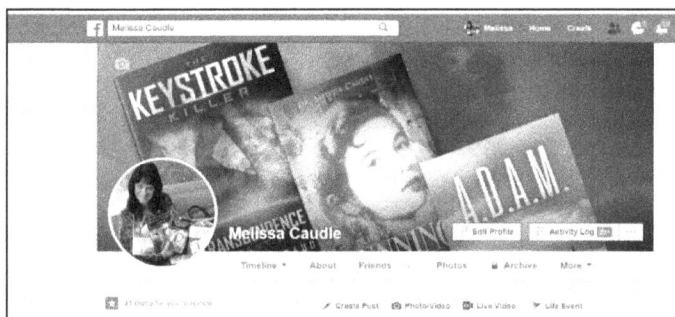

The moment I received the cover to my next novel, *Secret Romances: A Forbidden Thirst for Love,* I updated my banner to include it. I want to make one thing clear, this next banner not only highlights my novels but also the fact that I am an author. That is part of my branding, and I advertise my books too.

Take a Nap

Now you can rest, but only for three hours. Then back to the grind of marketing, but please stop to smell the roses and to celebrate your milestone.

LAUNCH DAY CHECKLIST

The Day Has Come and So Have the Nerves

Post on Social Media

○ Completed

Update Your Social Media Banner

○ Completed

Watch Your Book Reach as the #1 New Release

○ Take Screen Shot of Your Book as the #1 New Release
○ Email me your screenshot to drmelcaudle@gmail.com

Take a Nap

○ Rest!

Recheck Your Release Status and Ranking

○ Celebrate

8. POST LAUNCH DAYS

Although your book is published, you must continue marketing it and hopefully begin writing the next one. You must engage with your fan base and continue to keep the momentum going. Here are a couple of ways to keep your readers engaged with you until your next novel launches.

Join Forces with Other Authors

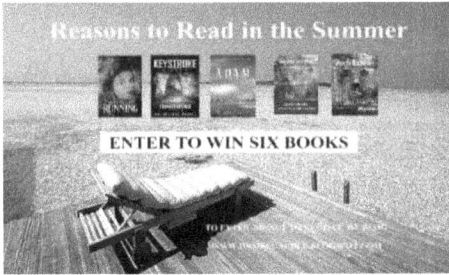

Take advantage of cross-promoting. Look for authors in your social media group that are in the same genre and run a multi-book giveaway. You could ask up to ten to join you. The success factor in this strategy is that you increased your marketing help by adding ten people to your team.

When they market the promotion on their Facebook page and other social media sites, they reach different fans than you, fans that may not have heard of you. This is what I call working smarter, not harder. Make sure to tag each author in any of your posts about the giveaway and ask them to do the same.

Carry your bookmarks

If I go to the dentist or doctor, I leave a couple of bookmarks by the reading stacks when I arrive. Before the nurse calls me, someone has already snatched one up and put it into their purse. I have also found that people keep bookmarks over business cards.

Begin Book Tour

When scheduling your book tour, make sure that you go to locations in the north, south, east, and west. This gives your fans an opportunity to see you.

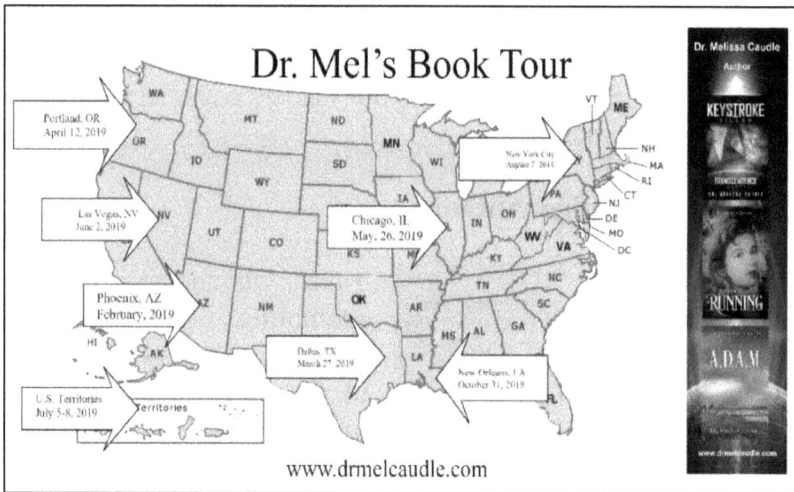

Create Seasonal Promotions

Mother's Day, Valentine's Day, Christmas, and summer holidays are perfect opportunities to create sales or for a brief time offer a free version of your book on Kindle. After the most famous "No Call" in NFL history, the New Orleans Saints fans boycotted the Superbowl. I live in New Orleans, and I am a huge fan. In New Orleans style, we threw a vast Boycott Bowl. I also offered my book *The Keystroke Killer* for free that day for anyone who didn't want to watch the game or attend the Boycott Bowl – instead, they could read my novel. It worked!

Not only did they download that book, they purchased *Never Stop Running*.

Research National Days and Promote Around Them

August 2nd is National Coloring Day, so I promote my six adult coloring books around that day and host a giveaway. For my book *Secret Romances: A Forbidden Thirst for Love,* I plan on hosting a giveaway for it on Valentine's Day. On Mother's Day, since my mother graces the cover of *Never Stop Running*, I plan on hosting a giveaway for it on that day. For this book, *How to Launch and Market a Book*, and since November 2nd is National Author's Day, I plan on conducting a giveaway on that day. The key is to tap into the national days according to your book's topic.

An easy way to discover national days is to visit the National Day Calendar website at https://nationaldaycalendar.com/latest-posts/. There are thousands of days for you to choose and you can even register your own national day with them.

111

Facebook Live Chat

Going live on Facebook gives your readers an opportunity to get to know you as a person by chatting with them so don't waste this opportunity. Once your conversations go live, you can add the recordings to your website and other social media sites. Your readers will want to discuss various aspects of your book and talk about the characters. A live chat is a fantastic opportunity to let your readers get to know you.

Also, if things get slow, have your book handy and read passages from it. Another tip is to have all quote cards and reviews convenient so you can talk about that too. Also, talk about what inspired your story and the characters. Get real with your readers because they appreciate it when you do.

Facebook Live Chat

Join me today as I answer your questions in this 'anything goes' discussion.

Today: 4:00 p.m. CST

LIVE

Answer Questions on Your Author Goodreads Page

Fans love it when they get to chat with you and ask questions. They can get down to the nitty-gritty of things. Get ready to answer the difficult and pressing ones.

Recommended Book Club List

When you're writing and want to keep your fans engaged, recommend other books to them. That's why I have my Dr. Mel's Book Club. If I like a book, I put it on my site, and I also add the link to purchase that book using my Amazon Affiliates program.

A book club list also brings in a different fan base from those other authors.

Take Your Book to Your Readers

I have found that no matter where I go, I can sell one of my books. If I am at dinner, I share with my server or those whom I engage in a conversation my business card or a bookmark. The other night my husband and I were at our local bar and restaurant when I handed a lady I had been talking with my card. Her jaw dropped as she stared at it. She became so excited because my book *The Keystroke Killer* just arrived and was sitting on the corner of her desk. Everyone in her office is reading the book to talk about it at the watercooler. I gave her several autographed bookmarks to give to her co-workers. I just happened to have a copy of *Never Stop Running* in my purse and gave it to her as well.

The following Monday I received an email from her asking if I would come and speak at one of their book club meetings. With that one exchange, I sold nine copies of *Never Stop Running*, and they intend on doing the next book club reading with A.D.A.M. Now that is eighteen books from one conversation and giving away my bookmarks. I call that a return on my investment.

This is where a large purse or backpack comes in handy. You can't sell your books when you out and about if you don't have them with you. Of course, you can always guide your readers to the book's Amazon page and have them purchase the book immediately, but there is nothing better than to have your book on hand and offer to autograph it for them. Again, this brings out the human factor and readers love an autographed copy.

I also make it a point to keep a couple of copies of my books in my car.

Set Up at Craft Fairs, Book Fairs, and Comicon

Again, it is vital that you as an author interact with the public. Craft fairs are perfect for this. A more expensive approach, and only if it fits your genre, is to get a small booth at Comicon. You meet thousands of people who want to meet you.

Take Advantage of Advertising Your Book on the Sidebars of Social Media Influencer's Blogs

When you advertise your novel on social media influencer's websites, you increase your visibility. Absolute Author gets thousands of clicks per day on their website. You can take advantage of their followers by purchasing an ad on the sidebar for your book. I would also buy an author sub-page as it provides you with a backlink to your website. They offer author interviews. Be sure to tell them that I sent you.

www.absoluteauthor.com

Also, my blog Dr. Mel's Message (www.drmelcaudle.blogspot.com/ or www.drmelmessage.com) has a massive following and receives hundreds of unique hits per week. For a small fee, I can place your ad on my sidebar too.

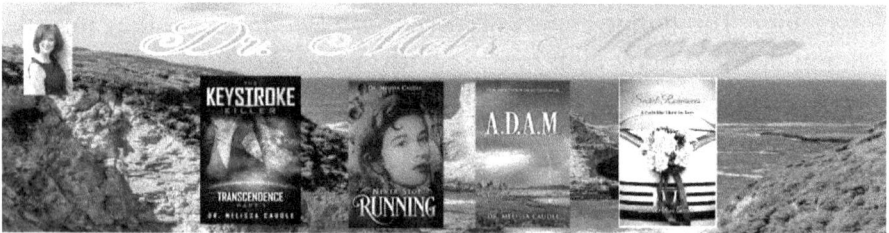

To find other blogs and websites where you can promote your novel, do a google search for "Book Bloggers." I have discovered that most have a contact form that you can complete and submit your request while others have a link for advertisements. Your goal is to find the blog or blogs that fit with your book's genre.

Tweet About Your Book

You can reach hundreds of potential readers by tweeting your book's information. So, don't miss this opportunity! The key to tweeting is doing it often, keeping it short, and engage your readers. Tweeting daily is essential and when you do, be sure to use hashtags with your post. Hashtags are critical as they help to draw potential readers to your subject matter when they search a specific topic.

Also, encourage others to retweet your tweet; there, capitalizing on the grassroots factor.

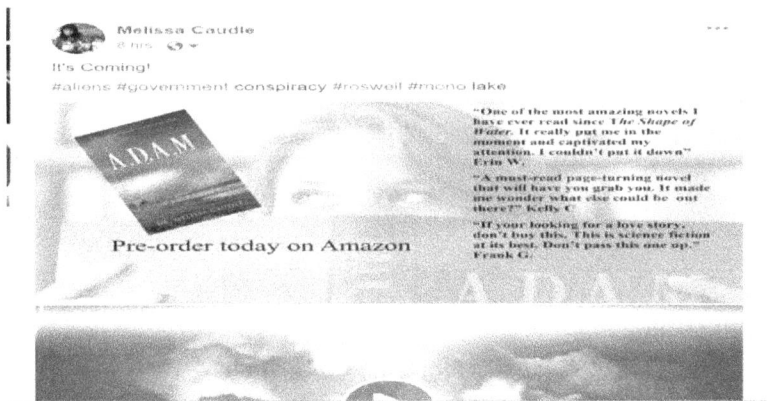

Have Friends, Family, Beta Readers and Others to Add Your Book to Multiple Listopia Lists

Anyone who has spent time on Goodreads welcomes the plethora of information available on novels and new releases. The minute your book goes live contact all your friends, family, and beta readers to add your book to Listopia lists. Readers search these lists for recommended novels. There are hundreds of listings so review them first and inform your launch team which ones you prefer they place your book on. You can even start your own list category. When you're logged into your Goodreads account, look for the Browse tab with a drop-down menu and scroll until you find Lists. If you click on it, it will take you to a page where you can search for specific lists.

From there, you can create a list or have someone add your book to it. If you want to check to see if you are already on a list, use the search engine.

After that, you need to blast this list and have everyone go to the page and vote for your book to bring it to number one on the Goodreads lists.

Issue Another Press Release

Maintaining a web presence for your book is essential. After the hoopla has settled from the launch of the book, write and distribute a press release to let people know how well your book is doing and add what you're currently writing. Also, if you have plans to turn your book into an audible, announce that as well. The more press, the better. Once released, be sure to place the backlink on your website.

My Web presence, 57,180 and counting.

Draft Articles on Your Subject Matter of Your Book Linking them with Trending Topics

Writing articles is an easy and effective means to engage your fan base. When you draft an article based on your subject matter, people who are interested in the topic will read it. The natural progression is that they find your book too. It's a win, win. For example, for my book *Never Stop Running*, the main topic is about my character's mental time travel through regression hypnosis where she discovers her past lives. There are lots of articles I can write for my blog that will attract readers who want to learn more about reincarnation.

Here are a couple of titles for articles that connects this novel.

What Does the Bible say About Reincarnation?

What Happens During a Regression Hypnotherapy Session?

How Regression Hypnotherapy Helps Retrograde Amnesia Patients

Now here are a couple of Topics for my novel *A.D.A.M. – The Beginning of Life.*

What Does the Science Community Think About Alien Life in our Universe?

Could an Alien Lifeform Exist in an Oxygen Environment?

What is the Status of the Arsenic Driven Microbe Discovered by Dr. Felisa Wolfe-Simon?

Sample topics for my book *The Keystroke Killer: Transcendence* include:

Serial Killers in Louisiana

My Interview with Derrick Todd Lee – The Baton Rouge Serial Killer

The Top Ten Serial Killers in America

The above topics came from my Keyword Search Tool which highlighted what people were searching.

Write a Series of Short Stories

To keep your readers engaged, provide them new material to read. Short stories are great for this. In fact, I started a series of short stories called Children's *Scary Campfire Stories.* These are short stories less than 1,000 words targeted for parents who camp with their children, camp counselors, Boy Scouts and Girl Scouts of America and church youth groups. Starting the first day of summer, I plan to post a campfire story in my blog and after that every week until the fall. This brings in a different target audience than my regular fan base. Therefore, I increase my unique hits to my website and hopefully generate more fans as they visit my blog and discover my novels. My goal is to generate sales of my books to the adults.

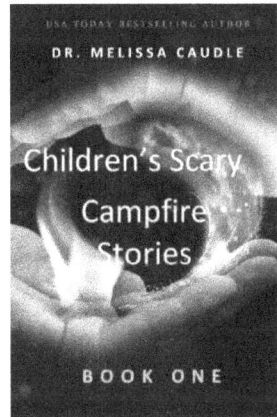

Although my novels are not for children, my real target audience is adults. The coolest part, once I have thirty or more short stories, I have another book by combining them. Oh, Happy Day! I've been writing them all year, so I have plenty to post, and I will continue to write these, and each summer publish a new volume.

Speaking of short stories, I have several avenues which target the audiences for my novels. Enthusiasts for aliens from outer space and UFOs as well as my fan base for *A.D.A.M.*, I can author short stories on close encounters. For the fan base for *The Keystroke Killer,* I can author short stories on serial killers, and for *Never Stop Running*, I can interview different people about their past life experiences.

Attend Live Expo's, Conferences and Networking Events

When you participate in a live event or speak at a conference, you increase your essential visibility. The more visible you are, you build up your fan base.

Develop a Workshop on Your Book's Contents

As an author, you can share your knowledge with others. This area is easier for non-fiction authors than it is for fiction authors. How easy would it be for me to develop a workshop on how to market and launch a book? Amazingly easy considering I already have authored the book. However, for my fiction books, I think I would have to develop a workshop on how to write a novel, writing without dialogue tags, plot development, character development, and so forth. The key is for you to figure out what you are great at doing and present it.

Use Your Vacations as a Time to Meet and Greet with Fans

I love the fact that as an author I can work anywhere in the world my life takes me. I travel all the time to the beach, go on cruises, visit Mexico, Canada, and many states across America. When I do, I make it a point to advertise where I am staying and invite my fan base to meet me at the hotel lobby or bar. I call them a "Meet and Greet."

It is a fun and free way to sign books without an official book signing. Of course, I carry books to sell. The best part is that I have lots of fun meeting new fans. Then you know what happens? They post to their social media sites that they met me. That helps spread the word about my books at a grassroots level.

Look at the fun I have had meeting people from all over the world.

Sign up to Bit.ly.com

When you sign up to Bit.ly, which is free, you can establish a tracking system to any URL including your book link on Amazon, your website, and your blog. This is an easy method to track the number of hits to your book or website.

Sell Themed Products on Your Website

Never Stop Running I think is one of my favorite novels that I wrote. First, I know the woman whom the story is based. That in itself makes it special.

Also, if you notice the emblem I use at the beginning of each chapter, it features a pendant watch necklace that in the story belonged to Gertrude during the 1820s and my main character finds in an antique store in the present. I have included that excerpt in my back matter for you to read. That symbol brands this book. I found a wholesaler who offered me two hundred of the same pendants at a reasonable price, and I sell them on my website and in my antique shop along with my books. The fun part was that I gave each of my Beta Readers one of the necklaces as a thank you gift. They loved it.

I must admit finding an item for *The Keystroke Killer* is a little trickier. However, I do have t-shirts with quotes from the book, coffee cups, mouse pads, etc.

For *A.D.A.M.* I have UFO charms, alien head charm, rockets, and t-shirts. Let your imagination go with the opportunity for your merchandise. Now here is the vital aspect of merchandise, when someone other than my fan base Googles "Watch Pendants," and "UFO Charms" my merchandise pops up and brings them to my site, therefore, driving them in the direction to purchase my books.

Cosign Your Book at Bookstores or Other Retailers

FAMILY TREE

ANTIQUES & TREASURES

Don't overlook your neighborhood bookstore or another retailer that might be connected to your book to cosign your book. Often, retailers might not want to take the chance to sell your book by paying upfront. That is where consignment comes in handy. In one aspect, I am fortunate that my family owns Family Tree Antiques & Collectibles in Bay St. Louis, MS because I sell all my books in that store too. Here is the kicker. In my novel *Never Stop Running* my main character visits this antique store so it is a natural tie in to sell my novel there. I place autographed copies for purchase along with other merchandise on the display case. Look at the picture below and notice that I have *The Keystroke Killer* and *Never Stop Running* on one of the displayed. Next, to them are individual antique marbles like the one I mentioned in one of the past life regressions. It all ties in with my novels subject matter.

The next picture is of the wall where I display the watch pendant necklaces I use to brand the novel. Again, when someone buys *Never Stop Running*, they almost always purchase the necklace too. Also, notice the items on the right; e.g., spaceships, rockets, and aliens. Again, marketing merchandise that is in place for my book *A.D.A.M.* upon its release.

If you are ever in Bay St. Louis, MS drop by my family's antique store and tell them you read about it in one of my books.

What if you don't own a store? In my novels, I write using local establishments set in New Orleans. Since I treat my characters as living and breathing individuals, they frequent restaurants, bars, and stores. In my novels, I identify them by name as well as provide a very descriptive detail of the atmosphere. Once I publish a book, I take it to the managers, show them that I mentioned their establishment and nine times out of ten they either purchase a book, want my autograph, and offer to sell the book on consignment. Sometimes, they take my picture with them and post it. I can't purchase advertising like this. Look for ways to add local icon businesses to your novel.

BEFORE I SIGN OFF

I'm sure there are many other ways to market your novel other than what I presented; however, I am confident that I have provided valuable information for you on how to launch and market your book. It may seem tedious and overwhelming, but these strategies work if you apply them. I have launched several books as the #1 New Release on Amazon by following the marketing strategy I presented. I wish you all the success in your writing career.

Also, please email me, follow me on my social sites and let's connect. Most of all keep writing. The more books you publish, the quicker your fan base grows.

Before I sign off, I would love to hear from you about your launch experience after using this book, and I look forward to seeing that orange #1 New Release banner on Amazon next to it. Please share with me your success by emailing me at drmelcaudle@gmail.com and sending me your pictures.

Happy Authoring!

POST LAUNCH MARKETING CHECKLIST

It's Not Over Until It's Over and It's Never Over

Join Forces with Authors

○ Completed

Carry Bookmarks

○ Bookmarks in purse or messenger bag
○ Bookmark supply in your car
○ Bookmarks in a travel bag
○ Bookmarks in computer bag

Create Seasonal Promotions

○ Identify National Holidays Your Book is Themed to

    1. _____

    2. _____

    3. _____

    4. _____

Facebook Live Chats

○ Search Amazon

Update All Author Pages

○ Facebook
○ Amazon Author Central
○ Goodreads

Set up at Craft Fairs/Conventions

○ Identify Three Avenues:

1. _____

2. _____

3. _____

Start a Book Club List on Website

○ Completed

Complete Author Interviews

○ www.absoluteauthor.com
○ www.drmelcaudle.blogspot.com/

Create Listopia Lists on Goodreads

○ Completed

Start Over and Author Another Book

○ Completed

Issue Post Press Release

○ Completed

Publish Subject Matter Articles

○ Completed

Write and Publish a Short Story

○ Completed

Attend Expo, Conferences, and Networking Events

○ Completed

Create and Hold a Workshop

○ Completed

Host a Meet and Greet

○ Completed

Sign up to Bit.ly.com

○ Completed

Sell Merchandise

○ Completed

Cosign Book

○ Completed

DR. MELISSA CAUDLE

ABOUT THE AUTHOR

Dr. Melissa Caudle debuted her novel "Never Stop Running: A Novel on Reincarnation" as the #1 New Release on Amazon. She is best known for her book "The Keystroke Killer Transcendence," a psychological thriller which took her to death row to interview serial killers. Her other novels include *A.D.A.M., Never Stop Running, Secret Romances: A Forbidden Thirst for Love,* and *Reborn.* She also has several children's and educational books including her new one *Scary Children's Campfire Stories.*

Her books have received five-starred reviews in Publishers Weekly, Booklist, Goodreads and on Amazon. She also writes non-fiction guidebooks for screenwriters on how to create a one pager, write a logline, write a synopsis and more. She also has a series of adult coloring books called "Abstract Faces."

"Dr. Mel's Message," her blog, has more than 125,500 views/followers where she writes about myriad interests.

She enjoys the city life of New Orleans along with her husband Mike and their two sidekicks, a Tuxedo cat named Meow Mix and an American Gray Shorthair named Simone. She retired from a twenty-year career in education after writing a number one best seller on crisis management which took her worldwide as a keynote speaker to educational conferences and entered the film industry where she experimented with various occupations: production assistant, director's assistant, travel coordinator, script supervisor, screenwriter, and director. However, she left that field in favor of pursuing her lifelong passion for writing. She does her best writing at her beach condo, on cruise ships, or in her sunny-patio-home office overlooking the paradise pool. For more information email her at drmelcaudle@gmail.com or visit her website: www.drmelcaudle.com. To keep up with new releases or speaking events sign up for her blog at www.drmelmessage.com.

MY BACK MATTER

Early in this book, I informed you how important back matter was to help you promote your book. So, I'm practicing what I preached.

  I wanted to share with you excerpts from my novels. If you like what you read, I would be honored if you read the novels and leave me an honest review on Amazon and Goodreads. Below are my essential links all in one convenient spot.

My Author Website
https://www.drmelcaudle.com

Dr. Mel's Message – My Blog
https://www.drmelmessage.com/

Subscribe to Dr. Mel's Message
https://mailchi.mp/49349c2474d8/drmelsmessage

Never Stop Running **– Purchase Link**
https://amzn.to/2U47jYv

The Keystroke Killer: Transcendence **- Purchase Link**
https://amzn.to/2ErQtgH

A.D.A.M – The Beginning of Life - Purchase Link
https://amzn.to/2H2ik9O

Subscribe to Absolute Author Blog
https://mailchi.mp/752e94da6e99/absoluteauthor

Social Media Sites
https://twitter.com/#!/DrMelcaudle
https://www.facebook.com/DrMelCaudle
https://www.facebook.com/The Keystroke Killer Fan Site
linkedin.com/in/dr-mel-caudle-650a4036

DR. MELISSA CAUDLE

AN EXCERPT FROM THE KEYSTROKE KILLER

Absolute Author
Publishing House

New Orleans – 2058 - MATTHEW RAYMOND, a private investigator, locked into a maze of deceit and deception uncovers the truth of Project Transcendence.

For Matthew Raymond, his job as a private investigator is personal. Extremely personal. After the disturbing 2053 murder of his sister Livia, Matthew left in a rage searches for her killer and answers to the mysterious questions that lurked around her death. Now years later, Matthew realizes his problems just went from bad to worse as he discovers himself immersed in a city where the wealthy and corrupt politicians rule. With his sister's murder still his focus, he finds himself in a cunning game of cat-and-mouse when he stumbles across The Keystroke Killer and uncovers a secret device capable of sending people to the fourth dimension without a trace. Project Transcendence becomes Matthew's new fixation. Searching the Deep South for answers, he uncovers family secrets, lies, corruption and a world on the brink of destruction. Can Matthew survive and save the world from the threat? Will he untangle the mystery of Livia's death? Find out in this compelling story, *The Keystroke Killer*.

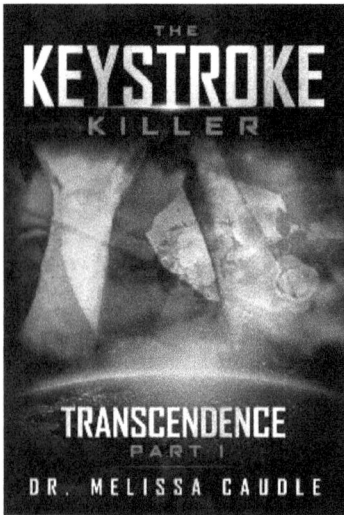

AUDIOBOOK COMING AUGUST 2019

Written by Dr. Melissa Caudle

Narrated by Scott Ellis

THE KEYSTROKE KILLER: TRANSCENDENCE

Excerpt from Chapter 3

There's No Place Like Home

Matthew rose and kicked the chair beside him. "Damn it." *Why didn't I listen to her?*

The desk clerk slid open the frosted window divider. "Detective Raymond." She waited for a response. "Detective Raymond."

Matthew's eyes flushed. *If I'd only gotten there in time.*

"Detective Raymond!"

"I'm not a detective; I'm a private investigator." He approached the door that led to a hall.

"Good luck in there."

A loud hum released the locked door. He stepped through the uninviting invitation.

In the middle of the hall stood two additional armed guards. The area consisted of several recessed secured eight by ten-inch lockers, a checkpoint station and an ironclad entry door that included an eye recognition keypad developed by Dimension Global. The door, dark gray metal six inches thick and eight feet tall, and how it sounded as it locked behind him made the biggest impression on Matthew over the last four years.

A loud buzzer, a clang, and a big bang echoed throughout the hall. Going out didn't sound as menacing. As he approached the guarded area, his heart raced, his temperature rose, and the tension throughout his entire body increased. He soon would sit across from the monster who killed his sister.

"Mr. Raymond, Check your weapon here." The husky guard remained alert as Matthew gently removed his gun from the holster.

"I know the drill." He handed it to him. "I don't like being unarmed."

The second guard pierced his eyes. "You don't have a choice if you want to visit Milo. Or, you could stop your yearly visitations."

"Not a chance. That shithead knows what happened to my sister. If it's the last thing I do, I'll beat the truth out of him."

"Don't you mean get the truth out of him?"

"Yea, that's what I meant. The bastard murdered my sister."

"Your sister was a victim of the Co-Ed serial killer? I thought you were the U.S. Marshall who captured him?"

"I should have killed him on the spot."

"Meaning, you could have?"

"Can I get on with this or am I the one being interrogated?"

The guard stepped to the retinal scan. The red light zipped across his eye and turned green. Click. The locker opened, and the guard secured Matthew's weapon.

Clang. The door slid into the recess of the wall giving way to the rancid urine smell and smeared dried fecal matter on the walls. The guards led Matthew down the unwelcoming hall. A faint whisper of burnt flesh permeated from the left, the odor of carbolic soap from the staff restroom on the right and the stench of unwashed clothes from the air vents filled the air.

Matthew looked at the visitor's restroom door. "I need to go in."

"Make it quick. Visiting hours are almost over."

***

The restroom door creaked as it shut behind him. Someone took a dump in the toilet and left it unflushed.

In the far corner by the janitor's closet, a rusty tin bucket served as the final resting place to an enormous and decomposed rat which reeked of rotting decay stifling Matthew.

"Disgusting people." *Did they leave their manners and dignity outside the gate*? He shuffled to the sink and scrutinized his reflection wrinkled by torment. A tear fell from his left bloodshot eye as he thought of the exact moment Milo slaughtered his sister.

***

Milo clutched Livia's hair as he dragged her into the Army green public restroom at Kenner City Park. The pervasive odor of urine filled the air.

Matthew in hot pursuit retrieved his magnum and sprinted toward them. He raced into the bathroom high on angered emotion out of breath.

Milo held a machete against Livia's throat as he grinned sinisterly. "You made it in time to watch your sister die."

"Let go of her."

"If I let her go, you will kill me." Milo taunted him as he pressed the knife harder against Livia's throat. "And, if I don't let go, you will kill me. Either way, you lose."

"Let go now!" Matthew's muscles contracted to know the monster before him would take her life.

"What will big brother do? Save baby sis, or capture a serial killer?" His ice-cold stare of gunmetal gray prevailed.

"Both. I'll do both. Put the fucking knife down, and we all can walk away."

"Giving up your vow to serve and protect?" Milo taunted to get a rise out of Matthew. "You'd let me walk, if I let her go? I think not. I must protest."

132

"I'll kill you. Put down the knife and let her go."

"Too bad." Milo slit Livia's throat and shoved her to the ground. "You're too late, hesitation kills."

Matthew lunged to save Livia. He kneeled over her and tried to stop the sprouting blood from her neck with his hands pressed hard against the wound. "Livia." Her eyes rolled back; she took her last breath.

Milo snickered as he watched the loving embrace between a brother and a very bloody sister.

"You're a butcher. You'll pay for this!" Matthew lunged toward Milo and struck the cumbersome machete from his grip. He heaved him against the cracked roach infested sink. Milo's cheek connected to it and split open. Blood smeared onto the sink and dripped down Milo's face. Matthew grabbed Milo by the shoulders and heaved his head against the mirror which shattered into several pieces and crashed into the pool of Livia's blood.

Milo snatched a sharp mirror fragment, charged Matthew, stabbed him, and sliced his left shoulder.

Matthew glowered at him, bent to deliver a reverse round kick, but slipped on Livia's blood falling backward onto his butt.

Milo laughed as he held back his mental powers to provoke Matthew. "I'm just getting started."

Matthew bolted up quick onto his feet and delivered a round kick. His foot connected solidly into Milo's ribcage cracking several ribs.

Airborne, Milo slammed against the wall. He grunted, took a deep breath, and charged Matthew.

Matthew outmaneuvered the serial killer. He dodged him, clutched Milo's shoulders, and used the momentum to propel him head first slamming him against the wall.

Bloody, Milo zigzagged toward Matthew.

Matthew rushed him, grabbed his shoulders, and butted his head against his forehead.

The room spun as Milo staggered toward his opponent. His eyes rolled into the back of his head collapsing next to Livia.

Matthew kicked Milo's ribs. He yanked his handcuffs from the pouch so hard it busted his lip.

Milo groaned and barely opened one eye, more of a wink.

A drop of blood fell from Matthew's nose onto the back of Milo's bald, tattooed head. Matthew dropped to his knees and handcuffed him. "I have you now, you son of a bitch. You will rot in Hell for what you have done."

Matthew kneeled by his sister, checked her pulse, and closed her eyes brushing his fingers across them. He stood and kicked Milo's face.

Police sirens blared as seconds ticked away.

Matthew glimpsed his bloody reflection in the mirror. He ambled to the sink and washed his face.

A light blue electrical power surge, originating at the overhead light fixture, radiated downwards onto the mirror which captured his attention. The blue light pulsated, zipped through the running water, across the metal pipes, and onto the floor to Livia's blood. Livia shimmered a faint blue as the surge entombed her. She became transparent and vanished along with her crimson blood.

Matthew became faint as he felt Livia's life leave her body. "No!"

S.W.A.T. burst into the restroom pointing their rifles toward Matthew. Matthew raised his hands above his head. A red laser dot centered on his forehead. Without lowering his hands, he pointed at the unconscious and bloody Milo. "That's the Co-Ed serial killer. Notify my father, Squad Commander of the New Orleans Police Intelligence Unit, Matthew Raymond."

***

Matthew exited the bathroom. The guard escorted him to the interview room at the end of the dreary hall. "You have ten minutes. Anything before that, knock on the door, and I'll let you out."

The nine by nine-foot room had a two-way mirror on the north wall. By mandate, Warden Stronghold and several guards watched the conversation between the rugged investigator and the ice-cold serial killer. The camera mounted high in the corner of the room reflected onto a bare bulb hung from the fourteen-foot ceiling.

Milo shackled at his feet and chained at his wrists sat on a metal stool behind a metal table. Both secured to the floor by bolts. A single wooden chair on the opposite side of the table near the door entrance awaited the interrogator.

When Matthew entered, Milo's hands pulled tight against the round metal restraint. He jerked the chains sneering at Matthew. "These necessary? I thought by now you, and I understood each other."

Matthew didn't fall for the bait unaffected by Milo's threatening gesture or posturing and calmly sat. "Had is the operative word. Why should I trust you without them?"

"You're not dead, are you?" *I could kill you with one thought.*

"The chains stay."

"Then, I don't talk." *He's an idiot.*

A standoff ensued as neither the interrogator nor the killer wanted to retreat. Matthew maintained the upper hand confronting Milo. He sat stiffly.

Milo followed suit. Neither man wanted to blink first as they glowered into each other's eyes. The silence roared until Matthew made the first move as he tussled his fingers through his scruffy uncombed hair. "Let me remind you of the position you're in. I put you here. I can keep you here."

The table vibrated as Milo scowled back unnerved. He responded to Matthew's emphatic statements by sneering more amused than intimidated. "That's supposed to make me talk?" Milo jerked toward the resolute Matthew. Only the chains that bound Milo prevented him from reaching his visitor.

Matthew didn't flinch. Not one recoil gave Milo the result he hoped.

"Oooo! I'm really scared now. Big brother needs protection by the chains that bind me. You're afraid to unchain me. Rightly so."

Matthew reached into his back pocket, grabbed a folded envelope, and pretended to hand it to the chained prisoner.

Milo gritted his teeth, grunted, and growled.

Matthew pretended not to notice as he dangled the envelope back and forth in front of Milo one inch out of his reach. "Open it."

"Not today." Milo desired to keep the upper hand.

"You scared of what you'll see?"

"Nothing in your show and tell game scares me." Milo extended his left middle finger and wiggled it.

A sneer crossed Matthew's lips; he didn't take the jeering bait as he placed the envelope onto the table out of Milo's reach. He flexed his fingers, folded his hands, and slowly placed them on the table. Matthew sat upright. "What I can show you should scare the piss out of you. It's from Nathan Hammer."

"You piqued my curiosity." Milo tried to slam his bound hands onto the table.

A lump formed in Matthew's throat as he secured the envelope between his thumb and index finger and lowered it one inch from Milo's shackled hands. "I'm not interested in what does or doesn't pique your interest." Matthew provoked Milo by fanning the envelope.

Unnerved, Milo deepened his cold stone stare, remained motionless fighting the urge to use his telepathic ability to suck air from Matthew's lungs.

The chair scraped across the floor as Matthew rose. "Maybe next time you'll show me respect and play my show and tell game as you emphatically called it." He strode to the door.

Milo sneered as he chomped his teeth to taunt him.

Matthew used his knuckles and tapped on the door protruding his middle finger. "Up yours."

Tap. Tap. Tap.

Unamused and unaffected by Matthew's blatant gesture, Milo leered toward Matthew. "Watch your back. That's, if you can."

"Meaning?"

"You couldn't watch your sister's. Now could you?"

Matthew turned toward Milo as his eyes trickled the calculated insolence of his stare. "You're not allowed to talk about my sister." He spewed spit with each angered word.

"You should have seen her face when I slit her throat." Milo gloated him further. "Oh, excuse me. You did." His tone in Joker fashion more befitting a character in *Batman* seemed to bounce in the room against the walls. "Such a thing of beauty to feel as her body jerked going limp before her last breath. Big brother couldn't save little sister." Milo smirked and tilted his head to the side. "I remember her sweet perfume and the silkiness of her hair." A grin of wry amusement dashed across his lips.

Matthew bolted toward Milo, grabbed the villain's head, and slammed it against the table. Blood oozed from Milo's nose. He pressed Milo's bloody face relentlessly on the table as if he had the strength of a Western lowland gorilla from the jungles of Africa. "You son of a bitch!"

Milo strained to avert Matthew's glare. His yellow stained teeth bloody.

"Where did my sister go?"

Milo's blank stare enraged an already violent Matthew.

"How did you make her vanish?" Matthew slammed Milo's head against the table over and over.

"Lost control big brother? I think so."

"You son of a bitch."

"That's the only name you have left in your arsenal? Low on vocabulary for a Tulane graduate."

Matthew slammed Milo's head three more times against the already bloody surface. "How's this for vocabulary? You're demonic."

Three guards rushed into the room and restrained Matthew. To break free, Matthew thrashed in their arms to escape from the three-person hold.

Milo licked the blood from his lips and sat up. "Tastes like your sister's."

A.D.A.M.

By Dr. Melissa Caudle

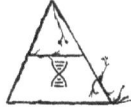

A scientist. An alien lifeform. A secret base.
Consequences for Mankind.

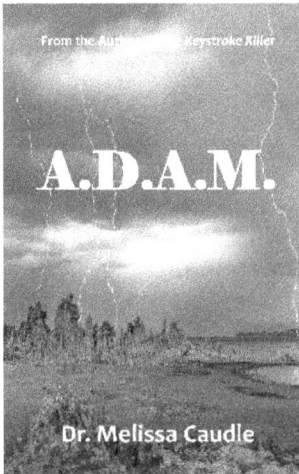

Meet Dr. Sandra Eve Bradford, an astrobiological researcher in charge of the A.D.A.M. Extraction Team who discovered a microbe which thrives off arsenic on the bottom of Mono Lake in California. General Anbar, Chief in Charge of the U.S. National Defense, orders his team to confiscate the samples and her research.

Dr. Bradford enlists her fellow researchers, Dr. Gregory Peterson, and her undergraduate assistant, Jessica Parker, to retrieve a new sample which set off a series of events and consequences.

In a government research facility, the microbe transformed into something alien. Once it becomes apparent to General Anbar the life form presents a national security risk, he orders his men to kidnap Dr. Bradford and holds her captive in an underground facility to continue her research.

The lifeform over a seven-day stretch, morphs into a human-like lifeform aging every moment toward death. His journey makes him question - What is life? What is love? What is hate? And, is there a God? This a story of possibilities and raises the questions - Are we alone in the universe? What else could be out there?

A.D.A.M. AUDIOBOOK COMING AUGUST 2019

A.D.A.M.
Excerpt

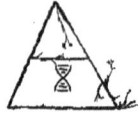

CHAPTER TWO – TRUTH

Dr. Bradford drove her hunter green Fiat on Interstate 10 from New Orleans towards Slidell.

Jessica twisted her long brunette hair into a bun and secured it with a pink scrunchy. "I'm hungry. I'm not waiting any longer to eat." She dug through a white fast-food paper sack that rested in her lap, retrieved a breakfast sandwich, and unwrapped it. The odor permeated through the car. Jessica curled her nose. "The eggs smell rotten."

"Get over it. Nothing has smelled good to you since you took in that mouthful of salty water at Mono Lake."

Jessica gagged, crumpled her breakfast sandwich back into the wrapper and threw it back into the paper bag. "You can eat yours if you want, I'll wait for lunch."

Dr. Bradford darted her eyes over at Jessica. "Give me mine."

Jessica dug through the bag and retrieved another wrapped breakfast sandwich and handed it over.

Dr. Bradford unwrapped it, took one bite and spit it immediately back into the wrapper.

"Told you, but, no! You didn't believe me."

"Please be quiet; let me think."

The silence between them ensued as they crossed the bridge over Lake Pontchartrain.

Jessica leaned toward the dash to stretch her back. "Are you sure it's safe to go to the lab?"

"They can't kill me in public; so, I believe it's safe."

"It makes me nervous. Let's listen to Stephen Stone Diamond. He's talking about extraterrestrials today."

"That's what we need, an alien conspiracy."

"I thought that's what we're in now." Jessica pressed the radio's knob. "It's not working."

"That's the best news I've had all day."

Jessica grabbed her phone and opened her blog radio app.

". . . Not just life here on earth, but also extraterrestrial life." Stephen Stone Diamond's deep and golden voice enhanced the mysterious topic. "It is unknown if there is any connection to the mysterious deaths of Dr. Gregory Peterson and the late husband of Dr. Sandra Bradford, Dr. Jeffrey Peck, who were both members of N.A.E.T. For those of you who don't know what N.A.E.T. is, I will gladly inform my listeners. It is a branch of NASA and stands for National Astrobiological Extraction Team. Coincidently, the research team led by Dr. Sandra Bradford. Phone lines are open."

Dr. Bradford slammed her fist onto the dashboard. "Damn! It's out on Blog radio."

"I'm Stephen Stone Diamond. I'll be right back to take your calls."

Dr. Bradford clenched her jaw. "Turn it off. I don't care to listen."

Jessica grabbed her earbuds. "That's exciting. E. T. phone home. I got to call in."

"Like hell, you will."

Jessica secured her earbuds, dialed the blog radio number, and waited. "I'm on hold."

"Jessica. Hang up. You can't bring attention to yourself or to me. Now hang up."

"So why are you doing a press conference?"

"The public needs to know the truth about my research. If the public gets wind of what I've discovered, they'll demand the truth."

"Well, in my opinion, that is exactly what Stephen Stone Diamond will do."

"Jessica!"

NASA Astrobiology Institute between the Louisiana and Mississippi border provided not only jobs but also fundamental research. From the spacecraft and booster shuttle rocket, the entry to the multi-functional compound reflected the nation's attitude about space exploration. Everyone wore either an official NASA or N.A.E.T. employee badge representing they worked either as an independent scientist on the National Astrobiological Extraction Team or a part of NASA. Visitors must sign in and wear visitor badges on their lapels too.

Dr. Bradford rushed toward the three-story "Carl Sagan Astrobiology Lab" which housed the N.A.E.T. lab. Behind her, Jessica, Rebecca Newcombe, and George, a camera operator quickly followed.

Without provocation, Dr. Bradford collided into Dr. Phyllis Gordon, a forty-four American scientist, and Dr. Edward Stolz, a fifty-two German scientist. Rebecca motioned for George to roll the camera.

Dr. Gordon's eyes pierced toward Dr. Bradford's. "You've gathered quite a following since our discovery."

"I'd have to agree."

"Too bad our samples were confiscated."

"This isn't the time nor the place to discuss this." Dr. Bradford strode briskly toward the N.A.E.T. research building.

The entourage followed as Rebecca motioned for George to continue to roll the camera. "What was all that about?" She caught up to Dr. Bradford.

"Common professional jealousy. That's all there is to it."

Jessica frowned. "I think not. It's about..."

"...Loose lips sink ships." Dr. Bradford motioned using her fingers as if locking a key for Jessica to close her mouth.

Jessica confirmed when she moved her fingers across her lips as if zipping a zip-lock baggy.

Rebecca glowered toward George. "Cut the camera. Damn it!"

The entourage barged into the N.A.E.T. building.

✦

The morning sun reflected off the five test tubes of murky water which rested on one of the lab's counters. A microscopic particle floated inside one test tube and for a nanosecond glowed neon yellow.

Moments later, the entourage entered Dr. Bradford's lab. Jessica flipped on the lights as she wrinkled her nose and smelled the faint musky and sulfur smell. "I'll never forget this smell."

The well-equipped lab included beakers, flasks, a Liebig condenser, and graduated cylinders showed the lab's importance. Most prominent, a silver and white 60X-2599X-2 binocular turret professional biological microscope proved essential in isolating micro-organisms. In the corner an assortment of lab experiments and three twenty-five-gallon tanks filled from the murky waters retrieved from several lakes labeled Lake Pontchartrain, Grand Isle and Honey Island Swamp filled the area. On the wall above the door a twelve-inch round battery-operated clock and a sign - "A.D.A.M. Extraction Team" marked the entrance to the lab. Each white cabinet had stainless steel handles which enhanced the sterile environment.

Rebecca tapped George onto his shoulder. "Be sure to capture everything in the lab. I want lots of B-Roll."

Dr. Bradford and Jessica dressed into their white lab coats, proceeded to the sink, and washed their hands.

Jessica prepped a microscope and a sterile slide. "I'll make sure everything is ready Dr. B."

"Perfect Jessica. Just follow the protocol. We have to get this correct." Dr. Bradford stepped to a locked cabinet, retrieved a bottle of arsenic and an eye dropper, and placed the items next to the microscope onto the lab counter. "Rebecca, it won't take much longer to set up."

"That's good to know. I don't have much longer."

Dr. Bradford retrieved the test tube which contained the particle. She extracted a sample as Jessica handed her the glass microscope slide. Dr. Bradford placed three drops of the murky liquid onto the sterile slide.

Jessica lifted her brow with excitement. "Isn't this amazing?"

Rebecca's frown deepened. "That's it, a test tube full of murky water and three drops on a slide."

Dr. Bradford defended her actions. "It's evidence that challenges the way we think and view life as we know it."

Jessica handed another test tube to Dr. Bradford. She filled the container using the water sample and gave the vial back to her. "Jessica, mark this sample A."

"Yes, Ma'am." Jessica looked at Rebecca. "It's in there. I've seen it."

Again, Dr. Bradford's posture became defensive. "You can't see it without the aid of a microscope." She filled the second vial and handed it to Jessica.

"Sample B." Jessica nodded with pride.

Dr. Bradford confirmed with a nod. "Remember, at its current state it is a microbe." She placed the prepared slide beneath the microscope as everyone observed and focused the microscope.

"I'll prepare the boiling water." Jessica predicted what Dr. Bradford would want as it had become standard procedure in the lab. She briskly strode across the room, filled a tea kettle, and set it onto the single electrical coil burner. She walked away but quickly returned to turn the knob to the on position.

As Dr. Bradford viewed the microbe under the powerful microscope, it vibrated and morphed into Dr. Bradford's eye. She lifted from the microscope, blinked, and rubbed her eyes.

Jessica noticed. "Something wrong Dr. B?"

"Nothing, an eyelash was in my eye." Dr. Bradford peered through the microscope and adjusted the focus again.

Rebecca's patience grew thin. "How did you obtain these samples? I thought the government confiscated them."

Dr. Bradford exhaled. "A few more seconds... There you are, look." Dr. Bradford stepped to the side as Rebecca stepped to the microscope. She glanced at Dr. Bradford before she lowered to view the microbe.

Dr. Bradford rubbed her neck. "Jessica, hand me my notebook please."

Jessica strode to Dr. Bradford's desk, retrieved a brown leather journal, and strutted to Dr. Bradford and handed it over.

The tea kettle whistled. Jessica at once prepped a beaker of hot boiling water and brought it to Dr. Bradford.

Dr. Bradford handed her journal back to Jessica and then placed five drops of arsenic into the beaker.

Rebecca peered through the microscope. "Honestly, I see nothing."

Dr. Bradford exhaled in disappointment. "My best hypothesis is the microbe transitions as fast as I isolate it. I'll isolate it again for you."

The two women exchanged places. Dr. Bradford once again adjusted the microscope settings.

"You never answered my question. How did you obtain these samples?"

"Let's suffice it to say I was on the extraction team and managed to keep a sample for further study."

"You stole it?"

Jessica came to Dr. Bradford's defense. "We didn't steal it. We went..."

Dr. Bradford lifted from the microscope long enough to glare toward Jessica and twisted her fingers as if locking a door.

Jessica put her hand over her mouth as she lifted her brows.

Rebecca annoyed at the silent gesture, huffed. "You agreed you would tell me everything." She gazed harshly at Dr. Bradford.

"I promised you an exclusive interview for a no question asked policy. When the time is right, we'll reveal our evidence and our source as to how we obtained another sample."

"I'll get another Emmy."

"I'll surely get my doctorate."

Dr. Bradford gave Jessica another cold glance.

"Well, I will. Won't I?"

The lab became uncomfortably silent as Dr. Bradford continued to isolate the microbe.

Rebecca tapped her foot. "Anytime would be ideal. I have a deadline for tonight's news."

"Patience, I almost have the microbe isolated."

"Yes, Dr. B always tells me that patience is a virtue."

"We go live at six. After the murder of your husband and Dr. Peterson, the world is waiting with bated breath to hear from the now infamous Dr. Sandra Bradford."

A reflective sadness came over Dr. Bradford, but she regained her professional composure. "You sound skeptical, Rebecca."

"Wouldn't you be? You claim to have evidence of an alien life form."

"Don't forget about me. I've seen it. Be sure to add that to your story. You know how to spell my name, right?"

Rebecca rolled her eyes. "This sounds ripe for a sci-fi murder mystery for *The Twilight Zone* and not the headline news story I wanted to break."

"I've isolated it; be quick this time." Dr. Bradford backed away from the microscope.

Rebecca quickly assumed her position and peered it as she squinted her left eye. "Like before, nothing."

"Maybe you don't know what you're looking for."

"Insults I don't need and won't tolerate."

"I didn't mean it to demean you. I apologize if I came across that way."

"Let's talk about the murders of your associates."

"I can't speak to the murders. I can only comment about the great men taken from this world. I was shocked to learn my husband was involved in a head-on collision and it was an accident. The investigators ruled there was no foul play involved. Frankly, I'm horrified Dr. Peterson was gunned down while on a boating vacation on the same lake where we made our discovery."

Jessica bit her lower lip and paced. *I don't like the way this is going.*

"Doesn't this frighten you?" Rebecca swallowed and leered toward Dr. Bradford with unashamed confidence.

"Of course, I am as anyone in my situation would be. You never know who your enemy is even if they stood in front of you as a friend. It's a cut-throat industry when claiming a scientific discovery."

"Especially one that's as big as this." Jessica beamed with delight.

A quiet knock on the lab's door caught everyone's attention.

Dr. Bradford looked at the samples and over toward the door as Jessica jumped and dropped Dr. Bradford's journal as a wallet size photograph of an infant tumbled from it and onto the floor.

FBI Agent Morrison, a handsome African American male, late forties, and Agent Turner an African American female in her late thirties brashly entered.

Jessica's eyes widened as her trembling hands went straight toward the ceiling. "Whoa, gun!"

Agent Morrison flashed his shield. "Miss, you can put your hands down. We're here to speak to Dr. Bradford. I'm FBI Special Agent Morrison, and this is my partner Special Agent Turner."

Jessica slowly placed her hands to her thighs as she glanced at the journal and the photograph. She retrieved the journal and set the photograph back inside the journal.

Dr. Bradford stepped forward. "I'm Dr. Bradford. How may I be of assistance?"

Agent Turner stepped forward. "Not in the presence of others. What we have to say is confidential. Everyone needs to leave but Dr. Bradford."

Agent Morrison put his hand in front of his face and grabbed George's camera with the other. "Stop filming. You're in that directive too."

George jerked his camera out of Agent's Morrison's hands and stepped backward to put distance between them.

Jessica stomped her foot. "You're telling me, you barge into our lab and ask us to leave."

"We're not asking." His stare, as cold as ice, seemed menacing.

"But, I'm her graduate assistant."

"I have Freedom of the Press on my side." Rebecca stood steadfast.

Dr. Bradford raised her hand chest high. "Wait, anything I have to say, they can hear."

Agent Turner stepped closer toward Dr. Bradford. "In that case, you leave us no choice but to take you to FBI headquarters. Please, Dr. Bradford, retrieve your belongings and come with us. It will be easier for all involved."

A silent standoff prevailed.

"I'll consent, but I want it documented that I am cooperating." Dr. Bradford gathered her belongings and headed for the door.

Rebecca motioned for George to follow. He pursued the agents and Dr. Bradford as they exited from the lab.

"Wait! Dr. Bradford, your journal." Jessica handed over the journal.

Dr. Bradford hesitated. "You keep it. Jessica, lock down the lab. Use protocol FRIC."

"FRIC?" Agent Turner's brow creased. "And, that is code for what?"

"Factual Research Investigative Control."

Jessica smirked in agreement. "Lock up the science experiment to avoid contamination. FRIC that!"

Agent Morrison looked at Dr. Bradford. "Come with us please."

The two agents escorted Dr. Bradford from the lab as Rebecca, George and Jessica chased after them. The door shut behind them.

In a few seconds, Jessica re-entered the lab and secured the samples. The murky water in one of the five tubes glowed neon yellow as the water vibrated around it.

She retrieved her cell phone and dialed.

.

DR. MELISSA CAUDLE

ℰNEVER STOPℰ
RUNNING

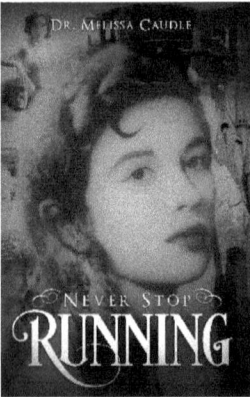

Based on a true story of one woman's struggle to recover her memories after a devastating accident left her with retrograde amnesia, "Never Stop Running" is an astonishing novel from an unforgettable author and is a must-read. What happens when the unthinkable occurs? What would you do if your loved one a suddenly woke up and didn't know who you were or for that matter who your family was either? For David and Jackie Hennessey, they had the perfect white picket fence life, marriage, family, and careers until the unthinkable happened - an accident that left Jackie with no memory. The couple struggled to find the balance between what they once shared and their new life. After David discovered Dr. Grayson, a well-known regression hypnotherapist, he convinced Jackie to seek his services to retrieve her repressed memories. During her sessions, her memories surfaced only to uncover her past lives which crisscross centuries in her mental time travel. Faced with a moral dilemma of believing the dreams were once a reality and twisting her religious convictions on reincarnation, Jackie questioned her sanity and feared for her life after seeing her deaths in her previous lifes. She believed she could never stop running as her marriage degrades and falls apart. Based on real events of hypnotic regression sessions of one brave woman, this is a tale of destiny and soul mates not to be missed. The most intriguing book you'll read all year. You don't have to believe in reincarnation to enjoy this tale, but it will get you to thinking about the possibility.

Excerpt from *Never Stop Running*

1. OPEN THE DOOR

Dr. Grayson sat in a Victorian chair; his eyes focused on Jackie who lay in a deep hypnotic state on a worn royal blue velvet chaise. The scar which ridged from her scalp to below her cheek covered by make-up embarrassed Jackie as she leaned her face against the pillow to hide it.

"From this point on, when I say sleep and snap my fingers, you will remember this state and go to it. Now breathe in and out." Dr. Grayson drew a deep breath.

Jackie responded to his suggestion with a huge-heaved sigh of relief.

"Jackie, I'm going to ask you a series of questions. You will not awaken but stay in this peaceful state. You will remain aware of your surroundings. Noises won't bother you. You will only respond to my voice. Do you understand?"

"Yes."

"Jackie search through your past and find a door and enter." Dr. Grayson observed Jackie's body language and eye movement beneath her eyelids giving her time to select a door. "Do you see the door?"

"I don't know which one to enter."

"The choice is yours. Think of a time in your past and open the door."

Her eyelids fluttered, her facial muscles flattened, and she looked more mannequin than human. Her right index finger lifted. "That one."

Dr. Grayson shook his head in approval. "That's great Jackie, open the door and step through. Where are you?"

"I'm in a scary place. I feel cold. It's really cold… dark… It's misty."

"Nothing can harm you, Jackie; you're safe. What are you doing in this place?"

"I'm in a dark alley."

"Are you alone?"

She barely shook her head. "Someone else is here… He's calling a woman's name."

In his hypnotherapist mind, Dr. Grayson analyzed her statement. "What name?"

"Gertrude."

"What is Gertrude doing?"

∞

Gertrude, age twenty-three, dressed in a 1880s overcoat with a silver-fox fur collar and a 1880s hat ran down a dark alley lit only by the orange glow of the oil street lamps and the blood moon. Fog graced the area as a light mist sprinkled. She tried to catch her breath. Smoke from the heat of her breath clashed with the cold misty night air.

A large man who wore a black Gothic cape chased her. "Gertrude! Stop! You'll never get away with this."

Gertrude ran to escape him. She tripped and fell scrapping both knees; the ground ripped her silk stockings. With the man in close pursuit, she pushed herself up and ran. She lengthened her stride as she looked over her shoulder.

Within an arm's-length of her, the man gained ground; he swiftly closed in. He lifted a butcher knife, lunged at her, and pierced her through her back.

Her body lurched forward as she fell in slow motion and landed in a mud puddle face down. The clammy chill of death gripped her.

He kneeled, rolled her over and jerked her brass crystal domed watch pendant from around her neck. She heaved as she took her last breath.

∞

Jackie raised her hips, wiggled her shoulders, and exhaled.

"Relax Jackie, he can't harm you; you're safe."

Jackie jolted. "He killed Gertrude; I saw him kill her." Jackie heavily breathed as her heart pounded against her ribcage.

"Jackie, what year did Gertrude die?"

"October eleventh, eighteen seventy-nine."

He pondered the date. "All right, Jackie let's move somewhere else. I want you to think of a calm, peaceful place, a beautiful place."

Jackie bolted up with her eyes wide opened. She put her hand on her forehead and heaved. "I don't want to do this."

"Please know you made extreme progress."

"I'm finished for today; I want to go home."

"Jackie, remember your subconscious has a way to deal with your fears if you allow it."

Jackie's voice cracked as emotions flowed. "It's just overwhelming." Jackie cleared her throat and held back her tears.

"I understand. Sometimes when we witness past events, we can become confused and scared. This is a normal process."

"I don't understand what just happened." A tear rolled down her mascara-smeared-scared face. "Who did I see die?

To be continued

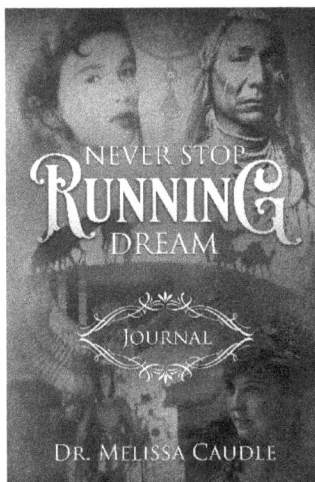

Available on Amazon

Never Stop Running Dream Journal
Never Stop Running Regression Journal

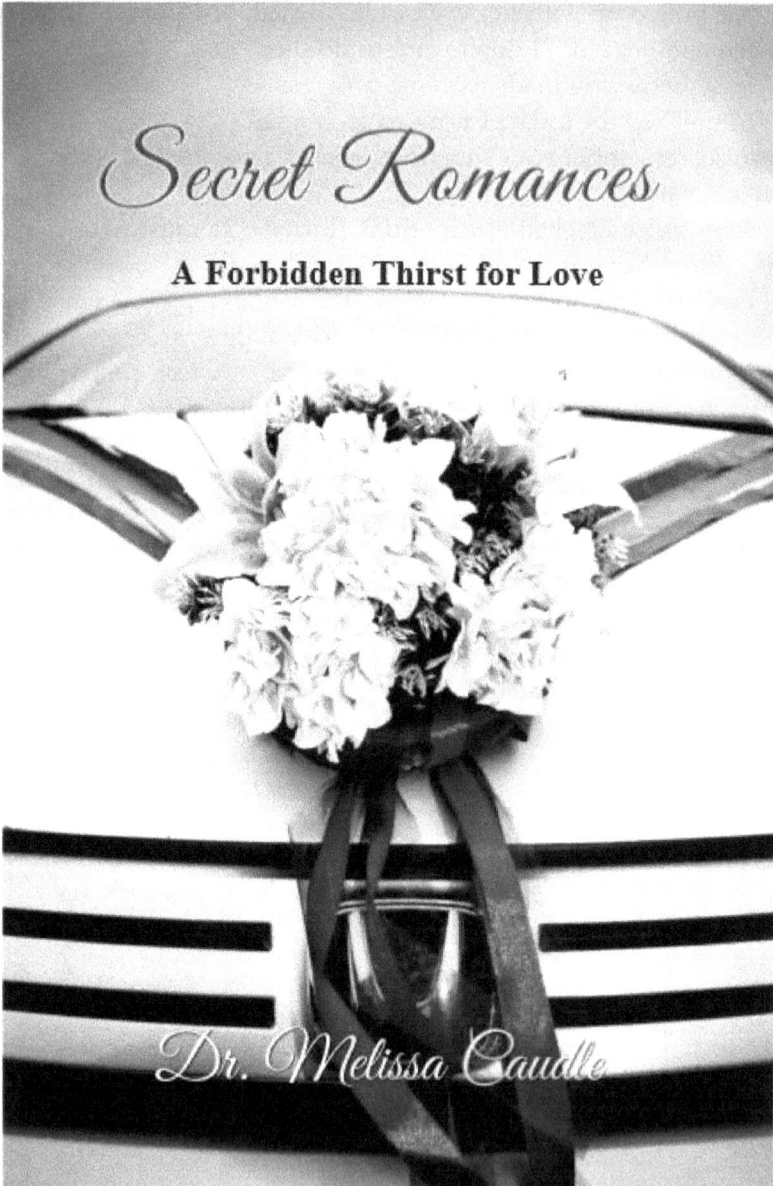

Secret Romances

A Forbidden Thirst for Love

Dr. Melissa Caudle

COMING FALL 2019

CHAPTER ONE

Fate

The downtown district of New Orleans, Louisiana bubbled with excitement along Canal Street. The morning autumn brisk air swept through Angela Whitford's long blonde hair as she made her way down the crowded sidewalk through the morning commuters. Everything about her said, a wealthy socialite, as she clutched onto her black leather messenger's bag in one hand and held her cellphone to her ear with the other. "I completely take that as a compliment, Dad. Your faith in me is what I always wanted. Take note the magazine hasn't fallen apart, and it's been four days since you turned it over to me."

From the way she strode toward the entrance of a high rise building to her prestigious Armani royal blue suit, she exuded confidence. Heads turned as she passed. Although forty-years-old, she didn't look a day over thirty. "Thank you, Dad. You don't have to worry. You and mom enjoy your world cruise. For the last time, I can handle the magazine. You've groomed me for this position since I could first read."

Angela stopped on the corner of Royal Street and gazed toward the sky rise building. A huge confident grin touched her lips. "Of course, Dad, if anything goes wrong, I'll notify you immediately." She took a deep breath as she pressed the end button on her cell phone.

The morning traffic heavy always provided a challenge to cross the street. In the distance streetcar, 941 approached. *I always have loved our streetcars.* She patiently waited amid the others as they tightly squeezed in around her at the crosswalk. She waited for the walking signal to flash white; and when it did, she scarpered into the crosswalk lane increasing her path toward her destination. The crowd on the corner seemed like one as they crossed.

A man in a Blue Bayou Cleaning jumpsuit approached and collided into Angela knocking her possessions out of her hands. His blue eyes, black hair and masculine jawline made him exceptionally handsome. "Lady, I'm sorry. Let me help you." He flashed an apologetic grin.

She drilled the man with a penetrating stare. "I think you've already helped." Her angry tone gave way to a brief smile at the corner of her lips when her blue eyes met his.

He quickly gathered her belongings and handed them to her. "Again, lady, I'm very sorry."

Several horns blew as the red light changed to green. An elderly driver stuck his head out of the car window with a glare of pure fury. "Hey, move out of the way!"

Angela face contorted to one of stunned surprise. "I guess we are blocking traffic."

He nodded and shot a wink in her direction. "Have a good day ma'am."

Honk! Honk! "Move it, lady!"

The man in the Blue Bayou jumpsuit strode quickly to the opposite side of the street. Angela clutched her belongings and dashed toward the high-rise building. She glanced at her crystal diamond Rolex watch. *I can't be late. There's too much riding on this.* She increased her pace sprinting through the rotating glass doors and into the building. The marble floors and golden brass trim glistened from the morning's sun.

The security guard smiled. "Good morning Ms. Whitford."

"Good morning, Charles." She briskly strode to the elevator and pressed the up-arrow button repeatedly. "Come on; I don't have all day."

Other businesspeople gathered around and waited too. Everyone seemed in a hurry for their workday to begin.

Finally, the elevator door slid open. Several people hurriedly exited as she waited for it to empty. She stepped in and pressed the button for floor twenty-three as several other others entered crowding the elevator like packed sardines. Angela quickly scooted to the back and leaned against the back mirrored wall.

The elevator doors shut and smoothly ascended stopping on the fifth floor. Six people exited. Angela stepped forward and snippily pressed the close button several times. The elevator door, slow to close, made Angela huff as she pushed the close button again.

The man who stood next to her frowned. "You know that doesn't speed things up."

"It might not, but it makes me feel better."

"Enough said." He stared straight ahead at the door as did she.

The elevator stopped on the eleventh floor. The man exited. "Have a great day. Go ahead and press that button since it makes you feel better."

Angela smirked. "What a jerk." The people's eyes darted her way. "Sorry, but he's a jerk."

After several more stops, the elevator finally reached the twenty-third floor. When the door opened, Angela exited immediately stepping into a lavish foyer. In the center, a forty-two-inch mahogany table which displayed a massive fresh floral orchid arrangement showcased the elegance of the office. She gazed at the impressive silver and royal blue inlaid 3D signage for *Elite* magazine behind the reception desk. An I'm-the-boss-now-smile pursed her lips. The floor to ceiling windows provided a perfect view of the city below.

She passed Monique, age twenty-four, a blue-eyed quirky, beautiful red-haired receptionist, who wore a Michael Kors navy blue cap sleeve stud trim Ponte dress. "Good morning, Ms. Whitford. You have several messages that I gave to your secretary."

"Thank you, Monique."

"My pleasure."

Angela made her way through the busy cubicle journalist area which buzzed as if in the stock market exchange. By the size of the workspace and the number of cubicles at least thirty people had started their fast-paced workday with publishing deadlines to meet.

Katie Summers, age thirty-four, and senior journalist stood as Angela passed. "Excuse me, Ms. Whitford. I have the article on the

Smyth and Smyth Architect firm completed; I look forward to your feedback."

"I'll get to it as soon as possible."

Katie shrugged in disappointment and sat.

Angela continued her pace toward her office as several of her employees who stood on the side engaged in conversation either greeted her or froze in place as if they did something wrong when she passed.

Francis Murphy, a beautiful brunette, age thirty-three, dressed in a Kasper sleek black dress and black heels met Angela as she approached her corner office which overlooked the Mississippi River. The plaque on the door read – "Angela Whitford – Senior-Vice President."

Angela stopped short of entering. "When is my nameplate going to be updated? I'm the CEO now."

"Hopefully today ma'am."

"Good. Please follow up on that."

"I'll make it my priority."

The women scurried into Angela's private office decorated exquisitely in teal and white as if on Fifth Avenue in a posh New York building. From the elegant glass desk to the sumptuous leather teal chairs, the office exuberated wealth and stature. When she sat, the Mississippi River Bridge loomed behind her.

"Ms. Whitford, a quick update. Your ten o'clock meeting with Mr. Morgan has been rescheduled due to a family emergency. I took the liberty to schedule another meeting with a new client."

"You did this without checking with me. You know I vet all our potential advertisers. We have a prestigious clientele. Not everyone can purchase ads in our magazine."

"I must confess, I did. However, it is for John Legions of Legions Airlines. Does he need to be vetted?"

Angela sighed. "I guess not, but don't make that a habit."

"Yes, ma'am. Are you ready for your interview with KWNC this morning?"

"I forgot about that. Of all days, why today? We have a publishing deadline."

"I believe it has something to do with you making the top list of the most influential businesswomen in Louisiana. Now that your CEO of one of the nation's top magazines, everyone wants to know everything about you besides being just a socialite."

"I get it, but I don't have time for this. I don't need to be marketed. If I wanted that, I'd put an ad in my magazine."

"Like you always say, there's no such thing as bad press."

"Fine, just give me a heads up before they prance into my office."

"Consider it done."

***

George Sidwell Preparatory Senior High school's gymnasium filled quickly with students sporting their red and black school colors as they made their way into the bleachers. At the end of the basketball court, four rows of chairs filled by the football team waited patiently for the pep rally to begin. Preston Alcott Billiford III, blonde hair and hazel eyes, sat on the front row sporting his number nine quarterback jersey.

At the opposite end, the band played the school fight song as the majorettes and flag team performed.

In one section of the bleachers sat the nominees for homecoming queen; each wore a magnificent mum with ribbons glittered with the words – "Homecoming Court."

Mr. Hayes, the sixty-year-old with silver hair principal high-fived several students as they entered.

Lonnie, a senior, looked more like a gothic-punk rock star in a school uniform than someone who attended an exclusive private school sat midway in the bleacher section next to his best friend, Conrad Pierce who also identified with the gothic-punk style. Conrad elbowed Lonnie. "I don't know what you see in her. Besides, don't you think she's out of our social class?"

Lonnie's brows creased. "Just because she's not rich doesn't mean I can't date her."

"I still don't see what you see in her. You're from old-school money; her family is dirt-bottom broke. The only reason she is here is because of the scholarship she received. I think they call that integration."

"Conrad, you sound like a snob."

"That's because I probably am. Like my daddy always said, it is just as easy to fall in love with someone who's rich as it is to fall in love with someone who is poor."

155

"You're a snob. When you get to know Jamie, you'll understand."

"I'm just saying, save yourself. You'll find a girl more suited to your ranking when you go to Harvard next year. You at least owe yourself that much."

The band's song ended as the flag team and majorettes took their seats on the bleachers.

Conrad exhaled. "Please pray that the Glee Club doesn't perform."

"Since when do you pray?"

"At the thought of the Glee Club. I'll take rock and roll any day of the week."

"Here they come." Lonnie pointed to the girl's locker room exit.

The cheerleading squad sprinted into the gym screaming, "Go Spartans!" Three male cheerleaders and the team's Spartan mascot dashed from the boy's locker room. Several cheerleaders performed backflips until they lined up in formation across center court. The mascot strutted his way in front of the bleachers as his red cape flowed. His fake gold Spartan helmet almost fell off as he grabbed it.

Conrad elbowed Lonnie again and then pointed at the mascot. "I wouldn't dress like that even if they gave me a million dollars. Oh, wait. I already have a million dollars. I'm a trust fund baby."

"Now I know you're a snob."

"A rich snob, but what male in their right mind wears a gladiator dress exposing his hairy ass legs? He looks ridiculous."

"You're one to talk. Have you noticed we don't exactly fit in either?"

"It's not because we can't. It's because we don't want to."

Conrad raised a rocker fist pump. "Rock on!"

Lonnie smiled at waved at Jamie Seamore, a seventeen-year-old senior with long curly brunette hair, green eyes, who held the position of head cheerleader. She stopped at center court several feet in front of the squad.

Jamie took her position as she quickly glanced at the other squad members. "Ready? Okay!"

The squad performed a cheer which included Jamie as the flyer at the end of the stunt. She flipped off backward landing in the male cheerleader's arms.

Lonnie never took his eyes off Jamie as the squad cheered their way to a dance formation.

"Is she still pressuring you about going to the homecoming dance tonight?"

"I've got it handled."

"I'm just saying, if you give in now, you'll always have to give in. Set your precedents early in a relationship."

"This explains a lot. It's clear why you don't have a girlfriend."

"I don't want one. I'm waiting for the finer women to come my way. It's called college woman."

Lonnie cupped his hands over his mouth. "Go, Jamie!"

Conrad elbowed Lonnie again. "Please don't embarrass yourself. Let's get out of here."

As the squad performed their dance routine, Lonnie and Conrad exited the gym.

Jamie's animated cheerleader demeanor momentarily faded as her eyes followed Lonnie.

***

Angela, self-assured in her stance, stood in front of the floor to ceiling window in the journalist cubicle area. A few feet away Francis observed as she wrote down every question Houston Meadows, a handsome KWNC male reporter asked of her boss as his camera operator filmed.

"Ms. Whitford, one last question. How do you intend on keeping the magazine's reputation now that your father has retired?"

Angela bumptiously pursed her lips. "My father would not have put me in this position if I wasn't ready. I have worked here for this magazine since I was sixteen. I started by scrubbing toilets. I delivered the mail. I served as a receptionist. I sold advertisements. I copy edited. I wrote articles. My father made sure I understood every aspect of this company. There isn't a job at this magazine that I haven't done myself or willing to do again. Our reputation as the nation's top magazine will maintain." Her eyes glared at the reporter. "Any more questions Mr. Meadows?"

"That just about does it. It's a wrap."

The camera operator switched off his camera.

157

Houston smiled. "Thank you, Ms. Whitmore. This story should air tonight on the evening news."

"I'm looking forward to it. Enjoy the rest of your day."

He nodded, and then he and the camera operator left.

Angela rolled her eyes. "Francis, that was one of the worst interviews I have ever had. The guy is a complete jerk."

Monique approached Angela and Francis with a message in her hand. "I hate to tell you I told you so, but I told you so."

Angela rubbed the back of her neck. "How did you know?"

"I dated him in college. He was a jerk then. He hasn't changed."

"That's not important."

Monique handed her a message. Angela glanced at it. "Great, simply great. Another appointment canceled."

Francis smiled. "Look at the bright side, that gives you an opportunity to vet other potential clients."

"I suppose you're right."

Behind her, a platform on the outside of the window dropped down with the man in the Blue Bayou cleaning uniform whom Angela collided into on her way to work. He smiled and waved at everyone. He grabbed his squeegee and began to clean the windows.

Several of the female journalists stood as they stared googled-eyed at the window washer.

Angela's brows furrowed. "What is everyone staring at?"

Monique grinned and pointed toward the window washer. "Him."

Angela turned around; her eyes widened. "You've got to be kidding."

Francis swallowed and sighed. "I love the way he washes windows."

Monique nodded. "He can wash my windows anytime."

"I agree with you, Monique." Francis waved at the window washer again. "I wish he could come right through that window and get closer to me. I want to smell him."

One of the ropes that held the platform loosened dropping the platform a couple of inches.

Monique's heart raced. "Oh my God!"

Everyone in the room now focused on the window washer. The ropes which held the platform loosened again jolting the window washer.

"He's going to die. We have to save him." Monique's eyes widened with fear.

Angela's clenched her jaw.

The window washer knocked on the window and yelled, but they couldn't hear him. He tapped on the window again as the platform swayed. "Open the window! Let me in. Please help me. Help." Only his mouth moved as the glass prevented anyone from hearing him.

Angela took a deep breath. "He's asking for our help. We have to get him inside before that thingamajig drops. Somebody, call for help." She tried to open the window, but it didn't budge.

Monique frantically dialed nine, one, one.

Francis bolted to the far side of the room toward the fire safety alarm system. She pulled it. The fire alarm sounded.

Angela threw her hands up into the air. "Why in the hell did you do that? He's not on fire. We have to get him in here before he falls. She continued to try to open the window as the window washer's face turned panic-stricken.

Richard Hastings, an overweight African American male journalist, grabbed a trash can and then ran toward the window. "Move out of my way. Step back; we have to break the window." He hurled the trash can in missile style formation toward the window. The trash can crashed into it but bounced back knocking the journalist backward hitting his head on the corner of a desk.

Monique bolted toward Richard. "That's not what I had in mind for men falling at my feet."

Angela took control. "All right people, Plan B." She raised the left side of her skirt exposing a black lacy garter belt, thigh high black stocking, and a leather holster with a semi-automatic gun and quickly retrieved it.

A bead of sweat formed across Francis' upper lip. "So, are you going to shoot him?"

Angela aimed her weapon toward the glass pane.

The platform dropped another couple of inches as the window washer's eyes widened. He put his hands in the air waving no and almost falls.

The platform jolted a couple more inches downward. It jerked and swayed more almost sending the window washer off of it. He tosseled but grasped the railing.

Angela waved her hands frantically for the window washer to slide to the left. "Move, I'm going to shoot the glass."

The window washer obeyed her command as he grasped the platform and kneeled.

"You're going to kill him." Monique put her hand over her eyes. "I can't watch."

Outside on Canal street, a crowd gathered as they gazed at the platform which dangled and swayed. People bolted from the building chaotically as if it were on fire as sirens blared.

Houston and his camera operator immediately acted by broadcasting a live remote in front of the building. "I'm Houston Meadows, and I'm live in front of Benson Towers on Canal Street. Moments ago, a window washer almost fell to his death. Stay with us here at KWNC as this story develops."

Several fire trucks pulled up and stopped in front of the sky scrapper. The firefighters exited their vehicles and bolted into the building.

A news helicopter flew over and maintained its position and several local news trucks pull to the side if the sky scrapper.

Angela aimed her weapon. Bang! Bang! Bang! The glass cracked. Bang! Bang! The glass shattered.

Angela handed her gun to Francis as Richard, and several of the journalists pushed the rest of the glass away.

Richard hurled the trash can toward the window making an escape path for the window washer.

Angela and Richard pulled the window washer into the office just in the nick of time; the entire platform fell as the people below scattered. Smash!

The window washer landed face down in extreme pain as a pool of blood puddled around his left leg.

Monique's hands trembled as she returned the gun to Angela. "I don't like guns. They kill people."

Eight firefighters and four police officers led by Sergeant Danielson bolted into the area. The Sergeant eyed the gun in Angela's hand. "Put down your weapon."

Angela stepped forward. "Officer."

"I said put down your weapon, now!"

Angela dropped the gun. Bang! A bullet ricocheted throughout the area sending everyone to take cover. Monique fell to the floor and rolled as she learned once in high school during a shooting drill.

The police officer approached Angela with caution as several paramedics darted into the room.

Richard grabbed his chest. "I'm having a heart attack."

Monique, now under a desk fainted, and the rest remained gobsmacked.

Two paramedics rushed toward Richard and immediately performed CPR. The others dashed toward the window washer as the police officer handcuffed Angela.

"You have the right to remain silent…"

"…But, officer, I shot the window. I didn't shoot to kill."

"Tell that to the judge lady."

The window washer opened his eyes. The room spun; his vision went in and out of focus. "Excuse me, officer. She saved my life. She's my guardian angel."

Francis, grinning, sauntered toward the officer. She flashed a smile and batted her lashes. "Now, officer, that man would be dead if Ms. Whitford didn't shoot the window." She glanced at the officer's name tag on his uniform. "Now wouldn't he, Sergeant Danielson?"

"Even if that were true, she discharged a firearm illegally. I'll have to take her in."

Angela pursed her lips. "Francis, call my attorney." *This is the worst thing that could have happened during my first-week flying solo.*

"I'm on it." Francis bolted to Angela's office.

Sergeant Danielson escorted Angela toward the door just as the debonair striking John Legions entered. "Ms. Whitford?" His golden-brown eyes bulged. He swept his fingers through his thick raven hair.

"This isn't what it looks like." *My dad is going to kill me.*

CHILDREN'S SCARY CAMPFIRE STORIES

As summer approaches, it is time for families to prepare for their vacations. One of my favorite things is to go camping with all three of my daughters and their families. When the sun sets, we build a campfire which begs for campfire stories. The first thing my grandchildren do is ask for me to tell them a campfire story. Of course, they want me to make them up. Therefore, over the years I have created dozens of campfire stories. This book includes those stories and is appropriate for children of all ages. From the *Creek Dweller* to the *Crystal Magical Land*, these stories engage the imaginations. Don't let the word 'scary' stop you from purchasing this book as they are cute scary and not horror creepy appropriate for children of all ages.

AVAILABLE SUMMER 2019

CHILDREN'S SCARY CAMPFIRE STORIES EXCERPT

The Creek Dweller

[This story can be told with an accomplice secretly positioned out of view from the campfire ready to say their lines at the end of the tale.]

Once upon a time there were seven children, six boys, and one girl, who lived in the middle of a bayou so big that it went on forever. Folks from the city tended to stay away because they were afraid of their cars becoming stuck and getting mud on their fancy clothes. Their neighbors stayed away too, but that was on account of tales which spread throughout on black magic. The legend said there was a spell that flowed through the roots of the giant cypress trees which grew in the bayou. The children didn't mind a little mud, and they certainly didn't mind seeing a little magic, that is if they ever found any.

One afternoon in August, when the swamp was so muggy that even the cicadas couldn't sing because their wings were too damp, the seven of them lay out across the veranda panting and fanning themselves hoping for a whisper of a breeze to cool them off a bit.

"I'm hot," cried the littlest boy, whose name was Aryc.

"Me, too," answered Jax, who was two years older than his brother Aryc.

"I feel like I'm in a big oven," said Roger, who was several years older.

"I feel like I *am* the oven," said Eli, who was the same age as Roger.

"Stop talking, everybody. The hot air coming out of your mouths is just making me hotter!" complained Stamatis, the next boy who was five years older than Roger and Eli.

"You're talking, too," Jayden pointed out. He was the oldest, and not in the mood for all this complaining.

Stamatis was just about to argue back, but Blythe broke in, "Let's go play in the creek!" She was barely older than Aryc but clever for her age.

"Yes!" said Aryc and Jax together.

"No," said Roger. "It's too hot to go now."

"Yeah, but we'll cool down in the creek, and by the time we get back, it won't be so hot out," said Eli.

"Wait, guys," said Jayden, "You know Grandma's rule."

The other children nodded, and then chanted in unison: "Never go past the creek after dark!"

"Right," Jayden said. "It's already late. We'll have to go tomorrow."

"Come on," Stamatis argued. "We'll just go for an hour and come right back!"

"Just for an hour!" the other children chimed in.

Jayden frowned.

"Please?" begged Blythe.

Jayden shrugged. "All right, just for an hour, then right back here."

The children cheered. They all took just long enough to grab their towels and change into their swimming trunks and swimsuits, then marched down the veranda steps and headed straight across the yard going into the woods picking their way over the roots of the old cypress trees and ducking under the hanging Spanish moss.

In ten minutes, they reached the wide creek which curved its way past their land. The water was green and slow, but Grandma had always warned them it was deceptively deep, and they must cross the bridge to play in the shallows on the other side.

Over the bridge they went, the littlest children holding onto the hands of the big kids so they could all safely cross the narrow plank bridge that straddled the shady creek.

When everyone reached the far bank, Jayden announced the rules. "No swimming, play where you can see the rocks on the bottom, and keep an eye on each other." Then he counted down. "Three, two, one... GO!"

They all jumped in with a mighty splash kicking up a big wave which rippled out across the green water.

The littlest ones plopped down in the water by the bank scooping up the muddy bottom with their hands and patting it onto their knees and shoulders, washing it off, and then doing it all over again. The older boys started a water fight, hooting and hollering as they chased each other up and down the creek slapping and kicking the cool water at each other.

Jayden lowered himself into the creek and drifted out to the edge of the shallows with only his head and shoulders above water to keep a watchful eye on the younger children. He checked his waterproof watch now and then, but mostly he floated in the quiet water.

Blythe amused herself by building a mud castle on the bank. The youngest boys gathered near the bridge filling each other's sandals with moss. The older boys participated in a cannonball contest to see who could jump off a log and make the biggest splash.

Suddenly, Aryc stood up. "Hey," he said. "Did you hear that?"

"I didn't hear nothing," answered Jax.

"I heard it," said Roger.

"Me, too," said Eli.

"It sounded like a little voice," said Stamatis.

"A weird, sad voice coming from that tree over there," said Jayden. He pushed himself through the water toward the great cypress tree growing from the bank.

"Shhh," said Blythe. "Listen."

They all got real quiet and from a dark hollow under the tree's roots came a soft, high voice, sighing over and over. "Nobody wants to play with me… Nobody wants to play with me…"

"Who's there?" asked Blythe. She waded nearer to the tree bending down to look toward the hole. "Who's in there?"

"Just me," came the voice.

"Who's you?" asked Jayden wading over to Blythe. He drew her back by the shoulder and stood between her and the tree. "Show yourself."

The voice sighed. "You won't want to play with me."

"Sure we will," encouraged Stamatis.

"Just come out!" said Eli.

"Sure," said Roger. "Come out and play!"

"Come out! Come out!" Jax chanted.

"Come play! Come play!" Aryc chanted.

Soon all the children joined in. "Come out and play."

"Okay," said the voice, and the children held their breath as they heard the water sloshing around in the hollow under the tree.

Then an eye appeared in the dark space followed by a frog-like face, and a slippery brown body of a creature about a foot long, like an overgrown salamander, but with one giant eye in the middle of its head emerged. It waded out standing on its hind legs. The creature waved shyly looking back and forth between the children with its one eye.

Blythe gasped. "Hello, I'm Blythe. Who are you?"

The creature paused a bit. "Well, I live in the creek, so I'm the Creek Dweller!"

"The Creek Dweller?" they all repeated.

"That's me, but nobody wants to play with the Creek Dweller."

"Sure we do," said Roger.

"What do you want to play?" asked Eli.

The Creek Dweller tilted his head at Eli. "Well, what's your favorite color?"

"Blue!" answered Eli.

The Creek Dweller's brown skin blurred, then changed into a bright shade of blue that seemed to glow in the late afternoon sun. The children all gasped, then clapped.

"What about you?" asked the Dweller, pointing at Roger.

"Green!" he exclaimed.

"Pshh!" said the Dweller. "That's easy!" Its skin swirled lime green.

Jax couldn't keep quiet. "Mine's orange!" he blurted.

The Dweller snapped his fingers and burst into a fiery orange color.

Aryc chimed in. "Do purple!"

The Dweller spun around and turned violet.

Stamatis stepped forward. "My favorite color is... plaid!" he announced.

The Creek Dweller looked up at him with its one eye. "A smarty pants, huh? Oh, well." He clenched his eye shut and put his little hands to his head and concentrated for a minute. Then his skin began to crisscross with red and green lines and little yellow squares. He jumped into the air opening his eye and throwing his hands up as he landed with a splash.

Stamatis shook his head. "Yep, you're plaid all right."

"Please, Mister Creek Dweller," interrupted Blythe. "My favorite color is pink."

"Certainly!" The Creek Dweller paused. "Wait!" He looked behind the children. "Someone else is coming."

They turned to see a long copperhead snake slithering across the riverbank toward them. Its scaly skin gleamed like metal in the setting sun.

Several of the smaller children screamed and rushed back crowding around Jayden in the water. They knew a bite from a copperhead could mean death out in the bayou.

The Creek Dweller didn't seem to mind. It waded toward the shore up to the snake stopping right in front of it. "Do you want to play with me?"

The copperhead reared her broad head back hissing as its fangs bared.

"Watch out!" screamed Blythe.

The Creek Dweller rolled his one eye. "Don't you want to play?"

The copperhead struck sinking her venomous fangs into the Creek Dweller's body, and then pulled back ready to strike again.

"Oh, well…" said the Creek Dweller. He clenched his eye shut and put his little hands to his head. His concentrated for a minute once again.

The snake began to twist as her mouth opened, thrust her tongue out without making no sound as her eyes started to bulge. Her eyes grew and grew moving to the center of her head forming into one giant eyeball. Suddenly, the snake's fangs fell out, and then she started shedding her scales all over the beach revealing her slippery-brown skin beneath. Four bumps appeared stretching out into short arms and legs with little blunt fingers and toes. Finally, a high-pitched scream of pain rose into the darkening sky. The pathetic creature slithered away whimpering as she crept into the underbrush.

In the distance, the children heard the snake sob, "Nobody wants to play with me… Nobody wants to play with me…"

The Creek Dweller turned and faced the kids.

"Are you all right?" asked Blythe.

The Dweller brushed himself off. "Perfectly fine! Now, where were we?"

"We were playing the color game," said Blythe. "And it was my turn."

"Oh, right!" The Creek Dweller climbed onto the bridge and stood up tall. "Your favorite color is pink, isn't it?"

Blythe nodded and grinned with excitement.

"What kind of pink?" the Creek Dweller asked.

"Pink like a gumball?" Blythe's eyes widened.

The Creek Dweller curled itself into a tight little ball turning a bright candy hot pink. "Or pink like a tongue?" He unwound itself and stuck out its long tongue at them which turned the same hot pink. "Or pink like a pig?" He pushed his nose up and curled his tail into a spiral making oinking noises as it turned the color of ham.

The little kids all giggled, and Blythe clapped her hands as she jumped for joy.

The Creek Dweller bowed in the setting sun. "All right, you're next." He pointed at Jayden. "What's your favorite color?"

Jayden looked at his watch stepping onto the bridge. "We have to leave. We were only supposed to stay an hour, and it's already getting late."

"Don't you want to play with me?" the Creek Dweller asked moving in front of him.

Jayden froze. He answered very slowly. "Uh, yes, I do want to play with you, we all do! But, uh, well…" He hesitated, looking at the sun setting over the trees on the other side of the bridge. "I think you should have your turn first!"

"Oh, okay!" said the Creek Dweller. It turned to face everyone, and his one eye seemed to glow in the gathering darkness.

"My favorite color is… Red!" The Creek Dweller gradually turned red as he grew taking the children in his arms. "You will always play with me."

The children didn't come home that evening or the next evening, or any other evening after that. The folks out on the bayou say that on a quiet night if you hold your breath and listen, you can hear voices out among the cypress trees. Some of them are those of small children and high-pitched, while some are deeper and lower but all of them always said the same thing over and over.

[If you're telling this story with an accomplice, at this point they should softly call the next line from the darkness, instead of you.]

"Nobody wants to play with us… Nobody wants to play with us…"

ADULT COLORING BOOKS

BY DR. MELISSA CAUDLE

One of my hobbies, other than writing, is drawing abstract faces in a Picasso kind of way. I put together my favorites in a series of Adult Coloring Books. You can buy them on Amazon, Barnes and Noble, and my website: www.drmelcaudle.com, and other online retailers. I also have my art for sale on my website and at The Family Tree Antiques & Treasures in Bay St. Louis, MS.

BOOKS ON FILM AND SCREENWRITING
WWW.DRMELCAUDLE.COM

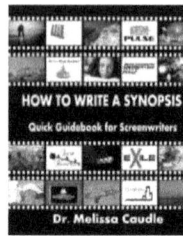

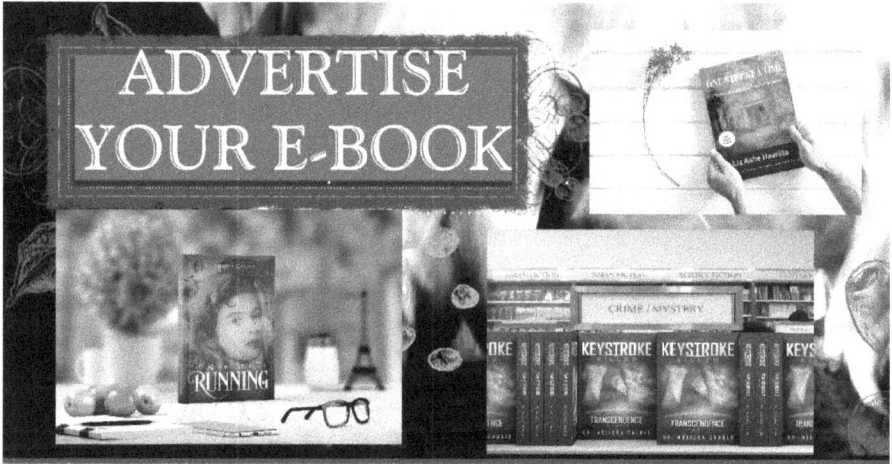

GET EXPOSURE FOR YOUR BOOK
BY ADVERTISING ON MY WEBSITE

Contact Dr. Melissa Caudle at drmelcaudle@gmail.com. As low as $5.

YOU CAN HIRE ME TO DO A CONCENTRATED BOOK PROMOTION THAT LASTS FOR 21 DAYS ON MY FIVERR FREELANCE PAGE.

www.ingramcontent.com/pod-product-compliance
Lightning Source LLC
Chambersburg PA
CBHW071532040426
42452CB00008B/988